THE HEARTBEAT OF HYTHE

THE STORY OF THE HYTHE PIER RAILWAY

ALAN TITHERIDGE

THE HEARTBEAT OF HYTHE

First published in the United Kingdom
in 2021 by Ceratopia Books,
2 Solent Road, Dibden Purlieu, Southampton, SO45 5QG

www.ceratopiabooks.co.uk

A catalogue record for this book is available
from the British Library.

ISBN 978-1-8384432-4-5

Printed in the UK by Cambrian Printers,
Tram Road, Pontllanfraith, NP12 2YA

Front cover photo credit: Zack Maynard/408 Photography
Back cover photo credit: Gary Woletz

THE HEARTBEAT OF HYTHE

FOREWORD

The Hythe Pier Railway was conceived and constructed to serve a specific transport need, namely, to transport commuters to and from their ferry to the shore at Hythe. It was built using a mixture of new and second-hand equipment that was readily available in the aftermath of the First World War.

As the railway approaches its centenary year, remarkably it continues to operate very largely unchanged using all original equipment, and still serving the primary function that it was built for. It is now almost unique as a genuine narrow-gauge public service transport provider.

Over the past 100 years, the pier and its railway have been subject to the vagaries of both local and international events, the Second World War, errant dredgers, and, of course, most recently a global pandemic. Alan Keef Limited has been involved with the Pier Railway for over 40 years of its life and continues to provide support and advice to all parties involved.

Alan Titheridge's book gives an insight into the railway's fascinating history, and looks to the future and continued beating of 'The Heartbeat of Hythe'.

Patrick Keef
Managing Director
Alan Keef Limited

This book is dedicated
to my wife, Anne,
for her incessant encouragement

and to everyone who has ever ridden
the Hythe Pier Railway.

From ragamuffin to royalty,
you are all a part of its history.

CONTENTS

THE HEARTBEAT OF HYTHE

INTRODUCTION

It is archaic, it is eccentric, it is a wondrous relic that has, against all the odds, survived into the 21st Century's throw-away world full of built-in obsolescence that we live in today. The Hythe Pier Railway trundles the length of Hythe Pier back and forth delivering and collecting ferry passengers some fifty times daily as it has almost without a break for a hundred years. One hundred years! There is not a person in or from Hythe who can remember a time it was not here. It has been abused, derailed, and more than once written off but this remarkable piece of early 20th Century engineering defies everything the elements throw at it and has embedded itself into the very heart and soul of the village. I do not know who first coined the phrase "Heartbeat of Hythe", but it perfectly defines the train's "clickety-clack" progress along the pier's not so straight track.

The purpose of the train is to get passengers over 700 yards along Hythe's spindly pier to and from the ancient ferry that links the New Forest village to the busy city of Southampton, a crossing of some fifteen minutes. There has been a ferry here since time immemorial. Some of you will have read my book "Hythe Pier and Ferry – a History", first published in 1981, reprinted and updated in 1986 and again in 2019. That book presents a detailed history of the Hythe – Southampton Ferry, Hythe Pier, and the Hythe Pier Railway. In this book, because of the inter-connection of the three, I have included a brief history of both the ferry and the pier but the greater part of it is made over to the story of the train. I have gone into the train's history in much greater detail as well as covering its technical aspect to the best of my non-technical mind.

People make history. Accordingly, I have looked at those who made it all happen and others who have played a lesser but still not unimportant role. The train is an anachronism that has worked its way into the heart of countless thousands who have used it and left an indelible impression on many of that number. I reached out into the community for personal reminiscences and was inundated with memories from far and wide, some of which have been recorded herein for posterity.

Sadly, although the Hythe Pier Railway is so endeared, it is suffering the ravages of time. It is looking somewhat dishevelled, more a favourite old sweater than a fashionable accessory, needing of some tender, loving care. The Hythe-based charitable group the Hythe Pier Heritage Association have an ambitious agenda to restore Hythe Pier and its iconic Railway to its former glory. The project is in its infancy but has the community of Hythe and district firmly behind it. 2022 will see the centenary of the train operating along Hythe Pier. Whether the intended restoration will be effected in time is now in the balance, but whether it is or not, a celebration will be the order of the day. It will be a time this little backwater sandwiched between the New Forest and Southampton Water will be able to proclaim to the world what a jewel it has in its locker. The Hythe Pier Railway is just that, a jewel, not just in its community but in the much wider field. It is a national treasure.

Train waiting at the shore-end station in the late 1950s

A BRIEF HISTORY OF THE HYTHE FERRY

There has been a ferry across to Southampton since time immemorial. For centuries hardy watermen and some rough old salts transported persons in row boats or sailing wherries. Largely unregulated, the wherrymen would take liberties with fares and there are numerous recordings of the flouting of basic safety with incidents of passengers overboard and drownings. By 1844 licencing was permanently introduced and order was established. Wherrymen in ever-diminishing numbers continued to ply the Hythe – Southampton passage until the early years of the 20th Century.

On March 10, 1830, Mr W.C. Westlake's "new steam-boat" **Emerald**, a wooden hulled paddle steamer, commenced calling at Hythe; twice in the morning and four times in the afternoon (with a trip from Southampton to Cowes between). The service was abandoned in 1832.

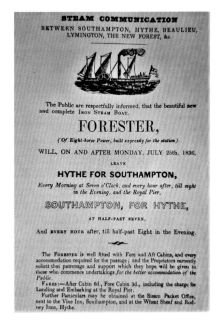

"The beautiful new and complete iron steamboat" **Forester** "built specially for the station" by Day, Summers & Co of Southampton, commenced operating a service on July 25, 1836 from Hythe to Southampton's Royal Pier throughout the day during the summer and autumn. The **Forester**, also a paddle steamer, owned by Capt. J.H. Knight Snr. and Messrs. Smith & Co. was under the command of Capt. George R Mason. This operation was also short-lived; by 1840 the **Forester** was being used as a tug in Southampton Docks and by 1844 abandoned on the mud in the Itchen River.

At this time the boats, both sail and steam, were using an old gravel hard that flooded at high water. In 1844, an Act of Parliament was given Royal Assent enabling the newly formed Hythe Hard Company to replace the old Hard with a new stone Hard which was completed in 1845. Under the conditions of the Act, the wherrymen had to pay a one penny fee for each passenger landed. This also applied to the next steamer on the passage, the "light and elegant" **Gipsy,** which entered service on August 25, 1845. Built at Northam by Summers, Day & Baldock, the **Gipsy**, also commanded by Capt. George R Mason, operated an hourly service in each direction. Patronage was disappointing, so a public meeting was called for on December 11, 1847 to rally support for the service but was so poorly attended it was decided to suspend operations there and then.

The Hythe and Southampton Steam Ferry Company was incorporated on July 17, 1855, and promptly placed an order with Day, Summers & Co for an iron paddle steamer. Owing to a prolonged strike, construction was seriously delayed so the company bought the wooden Thames paddle steamer **Prince Alfred**, bringing her to the passage in February 1856. The **Prince Alfred** had to be manually turned about by means of large poles between voyages. The company's new build finally arrived at Hythe in December 1856 and was christened **Lady Elizabeth**. The **Prince Alfred** was sold to a Mr N Harvey of Fawley who, for a short time, operated her alongside the new **Lady Elizabeth**. The **Lady Elizabeth** was simply too big for the service, frequently unable to get close enough to the Hard. Passengers had to be ferried to her by enterprising watermen in their small boats or sometimes even piggy backed.

Having disposed of the **Lady Elizabeth** four months earlier, the company took delivery of its second new steamer in December 1858. The **Louisa** was smaller and better able to reach the Hard, with a second rudder that gave her superior manoeuvrability, yet her owners still could not make the passage pay. The **Louisa** was sold to Mr William Winckworth on September 21, 1861 and the Hythe and Southampton Steam Ferry Company was dissolved on November 9, 1861.

Mr Winckworth had a second steamer built, the **Frederica** arriving from Day, Summers & Co in February 1863. Operating a continuous service with his two steamers, Mr Winckworth was the first to make the Hythe – Southampton Ferry a paying concern.

By 1870 conditions at the stone Hard were deteriorating, often requiring passengers to wade ankle deep in water to get to the boat. Plans were lodged for a dry landing pier in November 1870 but came to nothing. Further plans were lodged in November 1874 for a simpler structure by a newly formed company with the somewhat lengthy title of the Hythe Pier and Hythe and Southampton Ferry Company Ltd. Once again, the project stalled, but the company maintained faith and lodged further plans in November 1877. With finance in place, work commenced in the summer of 1879 and the pier took shape over the following eighteen months. On January 1, 1881, the Mayor of Southampton declared the Hythe Pier we know today officially opened.

In the meantime, Mr Winckworth sold the steamers and his interest in the Hythe – Southampton Ferry to Mr Frederick Fry on May 24, 1872. Mr Fry oversaw year on year growth in the passenger traffic, increasing the numbers from 92,000 in 1875 to 131,876 in 1883. In 1887, the Hythe Pier and Hythe and Southampton Ferry Company elected to put the pier tolls out for tender. Mr Fry declined to take part in the auction, the highest bid being lodged by Mr James Percy, thus starting a family connection with the Hythe – Southampton Ferry that was to last more than a century.

James Percy, circa 1913

Mr Percy acquired Mr Fry's steamers on March 2, 1887. He introduced his own new build in April 1889, the **Hotspur** arriving from the Plymouth shipbuilders Willoughby Bros to replace the **Louisa**. A second new boat, the **Hampton**, this time built locally at Day,

Mr Percy's first new boat, the Hotspur, 1889

Summers Northam yard, replaced the **Frederica** in May 1894. The **Hotspur** and the **Hampton** were the mainstay of the passage, supplemented by the steam launch **Hamble** from 1915 until the mid-1920s. Mr Percy had transferred his steamers to the family business, the General Estates Company, shortly prior to his death in 1915. Two other vessels, the **Southtown** and the **Yarmouth,** were brought down from Norfolk by the General Estates Company for a short while just after the First World War when passenger traffic exceeded the capacity of the **Hotspur** and the **Hampton**.

Under the leadership of Mr Thomas Bernard Percy, the General Estates Company ordered a new twin-screw motor vessel for the passage in 1926.

E. W. Mudge postcard, postmarked January 1911, showing the Hampton leaving Hythe Quay (Alan Titheridge collection)

The second Hotspur entered service in 1927 (Alan Titheridge collection)

The Hotspur II at Hythe Pier 1974 (Alan Titheridge)

The new **Hotspur** was launched on January 17, 1927, and entered service on Easter Monday, April 18, 1927. The earlier **Hotspur** was renamed **G.E.C.** and offered for sale. There being no interest, she was stripped of her engines and fittings and towed into Dibden Bay, where she was allowed to rust away. The second **Hotspur** was converted to steam in 1932.

Mr James Douglas Percy, who had succeeded to Managing Director of the General Estates Company, and a party from Hythe attended the launch of a new vessel to replace the aging **Hampton**, at the Rowhedge Ironworks yard on the River Colne in Essex on November 7, 1936. The **Hotspur II** was powered by twin oil engines and like the **Hotspur** able to carry 300 passengers. The wooden-hulled **Carrick Lass** was acquired from a Scottish concern in April 1937 to support the **Hotspur II** whilst a sister to the latter was under construction. The almost identical **Hotspur III** arrived from the same yard over the weekend of February 12 and 13, 1938, and was promptly put to work on the passage. The **Carrick Lass** was requisitioned by the Admiralty at the outset of World War II and subsequently lost.

After the war, the General Estates Company replaced the (second) **Hotspur** with the **Hotspur IV**. Similar in appearance to the **Hotspur II** and **Hotspur III** but slightly larger, the **Hotspur IV** went on to be arguably the most loved vessel ever to have plied between Hythe and Southampton, doing so until 2014. The

Hotspur IV after modifications in 1974
(Alan Titheridge)

Hotspur was transferred to Norfolk before being sold in 1962, when she became the restaurant ship **Hispaniola**, moored on the River Thames.

The three Hotspurs maintained the service for three decades. During the autumn of 1977, the General Estates Company announced an order had been placed with Hythe based Marine

Hythe Hotspur off Hythe Pier

Services Ltd for a new vessel to replace the oldest of their fleet, the **Hotspur II**. However, before construction had had the chance to commence the shipyard went into liquidation. The Portsmouth based **Southsea Queen** was subsequently acquired, arriving at Hythe on June 14, 1978. Repainted and with some internal modifications, she entered service in July. Her name was changed to **Hythe Hotspur** on September 25, 1978. She was predominantly used for charter and cruising work as she was found to be somewhat large against the Town Quay steps; accordingly, the Southampton Harbour Board permitted her to use the Town Quay pontoon whenever possible.

The **Hotspur II** was sold to the Clyde Marine Motoring Company, arriving on Scotland's River Clyde in March 1979 where she was renamed **Kenilworth**. She served on the Gourock – Kilcreggan passage until 2007 before moving on to the Moray Forth and taking the name **Kelly H**. In December 2017, after a cameo appearance in the 2016 remake of the 1949 film "Whisky Galore", she was retired and sold on. She was being used as a houseboat in the Hartlepool Marina in May 2021.

In 1980, renewed interest for a new vessel was brought about when serious issues with the **Hotspur III** arose, a dry inspection of her hull revealing major deterioration. Repair was deemed uneconomical, so she was withdrawn on October 31. **Hotspur III**'s register was closed on March 12, 1981 after she had been broken up on the mud adjacent to Hythe Quay. The new vessel was ordered from the Arun Yacht and Boat Company Ltd of Littlehampton. The **New Forester** entered service on August 20, 1982.

In December 1991, after more than a century, the Percy family, through its interest in the General Estates Company, sold the running of the Hythe – Southampton Ferry to Guildford based Derrick Shipping Limited. The General Estates Company retained ownership of Hythe Pier and its three boats, the

New Forester (Margaret Swain courtesy Sath Naidoo)

Hotspur IV, the **Hythe Hotspur**, and the **New Forester**, leasing them to Derrick Shipping. Derrick Shipping's tenancy was short lived, it going into liquidation on November 9, 1993.

White Horse Ferries bought the Hythe Ferry, including ownership of the boats and the pier, on January 1, 1994. The company introduced the catamaran ferry **Great Expectations** to the passage in August 1996, relegating the **Hotspur IV** to standby vessel. In 1999, White Horse Ferries disposed of both the **Hythe Hotspur** and the **New Forester**, leaving just the **Great Expectations** to operate the passage with the by then 52-year-old **Hotspur IV** as standby.

During the early years of the second decade of the 21st Century, White Horse Ferries found itself in an increasingly difficult position. The **Great Expectations** suffered regular breakdowns while the **Hotspur IV** was showing her age. In the spring of 2014, the **Hotspur IV** was taken off the service and out of the water, never to return, leaving just the troublesome **Great Expectations** as the only available vessel. Numerous vessels needed to be chartered by the hour as the **Great Expectations** appeared to be spending as much time off passage as on; these vessels included Blue Funnel Cruises' **Jenny Ann**, **Jenny R**, and **Ashleigh R** and Hurst Castle Ferries' **Solent Rose** and **Wild Rose**.

On May 22, 2015, White Horse Ferries introduced their Thames trimaran ferry **Uriah Heep** to the passage for a brief and a somewhat eventful career at Hythe. Not a favourite with the travelling public, in the main due to passage being confined to inside her somewhat claustrophobic cabin, the **Uriah Heep** had a coming together with the Town Quay pontoon on May 26, 2015, necessitating her withdrawal from service. She was taken to Saxon Wharf on the River Itchen for repair

Hythe Scene, formerly Great Expectations, approaching Hythe Pier in 2017 (Alan Titheridge)

and did not return to Hythe until July 16. On May 13, 2016, the **Uriah Heep** crashed into Hythe Pier, causing itself major structural damage. She was subsequently removed from Hythe, not to be seen again.

The **Great Expectations** continued to be unreliable. In October 2016, White Horse Ferries, through its subsidiary company Hythe Ferry Limited, issued redundancy notices to its staff, issuing a statement that it was unlikely to continue operating.

Blue Funnel Ferries acquired ownership of both the **Great Expectations** and Hythe Pier, assuming full control of the Hythe – Southampton Ferry on April 21, 2017. Very shortly into its tenure Blue Funnel took the **Great Expectations** off passage for inspection and overhaul, operating the service with the **Jenny Ann**. Despite occasional inconvenience caused by a much smaller capacity, Blue Funnel found favour among its passengers. The **Great Expectations** was returned to Hythe on May 23, 2017, sporting a bright blue livery and a new name, **Hythe Scene**. A new vessel, the **Jenny Blue**, was introduced to the service on May 15, 2018. Blue Funnel had supplemented the service with the **Oliver B** and the **Ocean Scene** on occasions in 2017 but now had two vessels dedicated to the Hythe – Southampton Ferry.

For the first time in a long while passengers travelling between Hythe and Southampton had confidence in there being a reliable service.

A BRIEF HISTORY OF HYTHE PIER

At two o'clock in the afternoon of Saturday January 1, 1881, the Mayor of Southampton, Mr J.H. Cooksey, dressed in his official robes, insignia of office and carrying his mace, performed the opening ceremony of the "elegant structure" of Hythe Pier.

HYTHE PIER Built 1880. 2100 ft. long

Hythe Pier, built 1880

A proposal to build a dry landing for ferry traffic at Hythe was first put before Parliament in November 1870 but its promotors failed to raise the necessary capital and commence construction within the two years stipulation of the 1871 Hythe Pier Order. Local promotors formed the Hythe Pier and Hythe and Southampton Steam Ferry Company Ltd, lodging different plans on November 30, 1874. This company was subsequently empowered to construct a pier at Hythe under the terms of the 1975 Hythe Pier Order but once again the two years stipulation wasn't achieved. Similar plans were lodged by a reformed Hythe Pier and Hythe and Southampton Steam Ferry Company Ltd on November 30, 1877. At the third time of asking, the dry landing, under the guise of the 1878 Hythe Pier Order was to come to fruition.

At a meeting at the Drummond Arms Hotel on February 6, 1879 a shares issue was floated with pledges for the greater part of the required capital already registered. The issue was over-subscribed leaving many disappointed when the company notified the relevant authorities that it was in a position to proceed. Messrs Bergheim & Co of London were appointed as the contractors with the distinguished engineer Mr John Dixon, who had experience of similar piers, appointed to oversee the project.

Pierhead scene, early 1890s

Work began on the abutment foundations during the late spring. Workers could be seen out on the mud close by the old Hythe Hard throughout the rest of the year. At the beginning of October 1879, the first of the ironwork arrived. An army of labourers was recruited, and erection of the new pier commenced. Further ironwork was delivered in February 1880, followed by the remainder and the

Hythe Pier, circa 1900

first of the timber for the decking in the early spring. The final pile was driven on June 29, 1880 when flags and bunting were displayed in celebration. By October 1880 all of the piles were reported as having been fixed. The new tollhouse was also at this time in an advanced state of construction. As 1880 came to a close, the new pier was ready for its first paying customers and the official opening ceremony.

Hythe Pier was an immediate success, its seven well-appointed landing stages allowing ferry passengers to land at all states of the tide. By the beginning of the decade following its opening, an anonymous contemporary account reveals that some "very neat wooden houses are erected at different points along the pier as shelter for those using it".

The same account adds: "An elegant, commodious structure will shortly

Hythe Pier, circa 1900

Hythe Pier, circa 1910

be erected upon the pierhead, embracing restaurant, waiting, music and other rooms."

In 1894 the Hythe Sailing Club fitted out a clubroom, subsequently extending the premises, at the end of the pier.

The facilities at Hythe Pier attracted numerous elegant yachts and their equally distinguished owners, particularly once the Hythe Pier Regatta, first held on August 15, 1881, became established in the Hythe social calendar. Both royalty and contemporary celebrities visited the pier during its early years.

On August 13, 1888, Prince and Princess Henry of Battenberg (Princess Beatrice, the youngest daughter of Queen Victoria) stepped ashore from their yacht **Elfin**, bound for a circular tour of the New Forest. After Prince Henry died in 1896, Princess Beatrice was a frequent visitor including on August 25, 1909, after landing on the pier from her yacht **Sheila**, when she attended a garden party at West Cliff Hall, home of Col. C.V.C. Hobart. On April 27, 1906, King Alphonso XIII of Spain stepped onto the pier from an Admiralty steam launch. The monarch who had been picked up from a Spanish destroyer anchored off the pier, walked the length of the pier to be received by Lord Montagu and driven on to a reception at Highcliffe Castle. The German Kaiser Wilhelm

II, who was staying at Highcliffe Castle, used Hythe Pier on December 6, 1907, to alight a launch from the German Royal Yacht **Hohenzollern** at anchor off Netley which took him on a tour of Southampton Docks before returning and boarding the Kaiser onto the **Hohenzollern**. Later in the afternoon, the Kaiser was returned to Hythe Pier from where he was driven back to Highcliffe. Prince Henry of

The Toll House circa 1905, Mr James Percy is standing on the right of picture.

Prussia, the younger brother of Kaiser Wilhelm II, and his wife Princess Irene of Hesse were guests of Lord Montagu of Beaulieu, landing on the pier on their way to Beaulieu on July 9, 1911.

Sir Thomas Lipton, a grocery chain and tea merchant as well as an accomplished yachtsman and regular challenger for the America's Cup, was a regular visitor from his yacht **Erin**. On July 4, 1914, he was on Hythe Pier with Signor Guglielmo Marconi, inventor of the first radio communication system.

Apart from the addition of the pierhead buildings and the shelters, other substantial work undertaken during the pier's early years included a complete end to end re-planking in the autumn of 1896. This work was contracted to Messrs Roe and Grace of Southampton at a cost of £1,500. In March 1909, tracks were laid on the north side of the pier "for the conveyance of luggage etc" on manually propelled trucks.

Major repair work was required after the pier had been struck by the schooner-rigged collier **Annie** on July 30, 1885. The vessel had been manoeuvring parallel to the structure on her way to Hythe Quay when a miscalculation in the lowering of the sails brought her into contact at about the mid-point on the north side. Five of the pier's cylindrical piles were either broken or carried away altogether. In 1915, the sailing barge **Itchen** came into contact with the pier, losing her top mast but causing no damage to the pier itself.

Immediately after the First World War, tracks were laid on the southern side of the pier for the electric railway introduced in 1922 (see separate chapter).

On February 19, 1921, the Royal Motor Yacht Club which had just taken up residence in the clubhouse formerly rented by the Hythe Yacht Club and subsequently the YMCA, published plans of proposed

The pierhead pontoon after re-positioning in 1947

additions to the premises which included "comfortable and roomy quarters . . . including a large dining room, galley, bar and four sleeping cabins" as well as a bathroom. These modifications were carried out in time for the 1922 racing season.

There had been a pontoon, designed by Hythe resident and naval architect C.P. Clayton, since the early days of the pier but in the summer of 1931 a new pontoon, roller bridged to cater for tidal differences, was introduced. This was first employed by the steamers to land and embark passengers on July 8, 1931. By this time the landing stages along the length of the structure were no longer in use. The pontoon was moved 12 feet 3 inches further away from the pierhead at the end of 1947 when reconstruction work on the pierhead that would add five feet to the pier's length encountered some old dolphin stumps just below the mud level on the site of the pontoon. This was done so that in the event of the pontoon grounding it would be clear of this potential hazard. So far as can be traced this pontoon survived into the 21st Century before a new pontoon built by Manor Marine of Poole was installed on August 18, 2002. A new fibreglass roof with internal lighting was subsequently added to the ramp.

During the Second World War there was a spotlight on the end of the pier.

A major refurbishment and reconstruction of the pierhead buildings was carried out during 1971. A canopy with corrugated Perspex panels with the legend "Hythe Pier" on the seaward fascia was installed across the decking between the pierhead buildings. A low platform was added to make the stepping into or out of the train easier. The paintwork was changed from the cream it had been for

Pierhead refurbishment, 1971 (Alan Titheridge)

the greater part of its existence to a dark blue and white, similar to that applied to the "Hotspur" boats and the train during the mid-late 1960s. The building on the south side that had been used as a restaurant for a number of years was given a facelift by its proprietors by changing the fenestration from small to large picture windows, allowing diners an unparalleled view down Southampton Water.

During the 1970s and 1980s the pier continued to serve the ferry without any further alteration or development. However, there were incidents which changed how it was used otherwise. Persistent vandalism during the early 1970s resulted in it being closed overnight from the end of May 1974, disappointing night fishermen. Fishing from the pier had been an almost everyday activity since its opening but the night ban was extended to a complete ban during the 1980s.

Fire is a constant risk on wooden structures with incidents reported in August 1976, July 1979 and August 1983, all related to discarded cigarettes. A smoking ban on the pier train was imposed in January 1986 and following another incident in July 1987, subsequently on the pier itself.

Between 1984 and 1988 major repair work on the shore-end and middle section trusses were effected at a cost of £290,000.

Ownership of Hythe Pier passed to White Horse Ferries in January 1994. With the pierhead buildings showing distinct signs of deterioration, the new owners set in motion a "rolling programme of refurbishments" in 1996. By December 1997 there was little evidence of any real improvement, with local councils applying pressure on the owner to carry out the improvements that it put at a cost of £600,000. In May 1998 a "sponsor a plank" scheme was put forward, proving a great success. With council support and a sizeable infusion of funds from White Horse Ferries, re-planking of the decking was carried out over the following few years. In April 2001 a council grant of £400,000 enabled further repairs to the railway track, improvements to the lighting and the provision of new safety railings.

On April 26, 2002, a "freak gust of wind" sent the **Hotspur IV** crashing into the northern side of the pier. Not only was the ferry boat damaged but so too was the pier, to the cost of £30,000. Two supporting piles about 50 metres from the seaward end of the structure were broken and needed replacing. A piling rig was brought in to effect the work. New RSJ beams were fixed to add support, while latticework also had to be renewed.

Damage to Hythe Pier, the result of the Donald Redford collision on November 1, 2003 (Photos: Sath Naidoo)

During the early evening of November 1, 2003, the dredger **Donald Redford** crashed into the northern side of Hythe Pier just minutes after the ferry-boats **Great Expectations** and **Hotspur IV** had disembarked their passengers and the train had passed by, leaving a gaping 80 feet hole in the structure, rendering it totally unusable. Despite financial wrangling with the dredger owners and insurers, the clearing of the wreckage to allow for the repair work commenced as soon as the various agencies completed their investigations. After much negotiation, occasionally public, insurers and the dredger's owners agreed to cover the £300,000 repair costs.

Damage to Hythe Pier, the result of the Donald Redford collision on November 1, 2003 (Sath Naidoo)

After a floating crane had removed the debris of the impacted section, leaving the pier in two very separated sections, the old piles were extracted, and new ones driven in. Lattice beams were repaired and reconnected, tie beams replaced, the decking and railway track was re-laid with the live rail reconnected. The impact of the collision blew the electric rail transformer, resulting in a replacement having to be specially made and installed over the weekend of January 3-4, 2004.
A ceremony to reopen the pier was held on January 8, 2004. A plaque is mounted at the point the dredger struck the pier.

White Horse Ferries' vessel **Uriah Heep** crashed into the pier, wedging itself under the structure, during the evening of Friday May 13, 2016. The ferryboat, which had only been operating on the service a short while, suffered major damage and had to be dragged out. Fortunately, no serious damage was inflicted upon the pier structure, but it had to be closed for 48 hours whilst an investigation and an inspection was carried out.

In October 2016, White Horse Ferries announced it was unlikely to continue its operating of the Hythe Ferry. This sparked an amazing response from the public of Hythe. Protests, petitions and the public outcry brought about the formation of the charitable organisation, the Hythe Pier Heritage Association that set out to actively raise awareness and the funds to restore Hythe's jewel that by the end of the second decade of the 21st Century was looking somewhat sad and forlorn. In May

*A facelift for the pier entrance May 2019
(Alan Titheridge)*

2019 the Hythe Pier Heritage Association was able to make its first improvement, giving the pier entrance a sprucing up with new signage.

Ownership of Hythe Pier passed into the hands of Blue Funnel Ferries, when it purchased the Hythe Ferry operation on April 21, 2017.

APPENDIX

Builders: Messrs. Bergheim & Co., London

Designer: Mr. James Wright C.E., 10, Cornwall, London

Engineer: Mr. John Dixon

Construction: 1879-1880 (Official opening January 1, 1881)

Statistics: Length, (approx.) 2,100 feet
Width (of pier proper) 16 feet
Surface Area (including pierhead) – approx. 36,000 square feet.
Height above high water – 4 feet (subject to normal tides)

Design: "The pier is composed of a pair of longitudinal wrought iron open girders, resting upon groups of cast-iron screw piles, 40 feet apart, and well tied by diagonal and other braces, the girders themselves being held together with cross girders of nearly equal strength." The deck was originally "formed of best pine joists, having the planks forming the floor, running in the direction of its length." It has been relayed on numerous occasions, usually with "best English oak".

Contract Price: £7,700

THE HEARTBEAT OF HYTHE

BEFORE THE TRAIN

There was a provision in the 1878 Hythe Pier Order for a tramway on Hythe Pier, but nothing was to come of this for almost three decades.

The Hampshire Independent for February 20, 1909, reported: "It is intended to lay down a tramway on Hythe Pier between the pier gates and the pierhead for the conveyance of luggage etc. as the passage with the trucks cause the planking of the pier to be quickly worn out. The contract for the work of laying the tramway has been secured by Mr E.J. Kingham of Hythe and it is understood that it will be commenced shortly."

Prior to this, luggage and goods were transported by hand carts with solid metal-rimmed wheels, as reported by the Hampshire Independent, detrimentally to the decking timbers.

A metal wheeled handcart can be seen in this early photograph of Hythe from the pier (Alan Titheridge collection)

Mr Edward James Kingham was a local builder as well as being the local undertaker. He was born in Marchwood in 1862 and moved to Hythe in 1897. He died in January 1937 at his home at Marsh House, Hythe, aged

Mr Kingham's tracks on the northern side of the pier decking

This Mudge postcard (postmarked June 11, 1914) shows a busy scene on the pier. Passengers and a heavily laden trolley on the tracks wait for the Hampton arriving alongside (Alan Titheridge collection)

74, leaving a widow, Mary, and two daughters. Both his sons died of war related injuries.

Work on sinking the track between planks on the northern side of the pier commenced in early March.

The Hampshire Independent for May 1, 1909, commented: "The work of laying the tramway on Hythe Pier for the conveyance of luggage, goods, parcels, etc, is making very satisfactory progress." In the June 26, 1909, edition, it was reported: "The tramway on Hythe Pier has now been completed but it has not yet been brought into general use."

On July 31, 1909, the Hampshire Independent was finally able to report: "The new tramway on the pier is now in use and luggage and goods are conveyed up and down on a couple of up-to-date trolleys." The sturdy metal four-wheeled trolleys were hand-propelled by porters. They were designated to carry luggage, goods, and parcels but on occasion a few people rode alongside their luggage. There was a turntable at the shore end of the pier.

The Southern Evening Echo for August 30, 1977, featured vintage photographs of Hythe Pier and the Ferry, clearly showing the tramway tracks, prompting a letter from 77-year-old Eva Elholt of Shirley, Southampton, published in the same newspaper on September 9, 1977, in which the former Fawley resident recalled: "I distinctly remember seats for about six passengers on lines and pushed by a rather fat man." She continued: "It was a great help to women loaded with shopping and I know my mother used it and I rather fancy I rode on it as a child but I'm not certain about that."

Passengers being pushed along the new tramway

It was reported in the February 12, 1910, edition of the Hampshire Independent: "The tramway laid down on the pier for the conveyance of heavy goods and passenger's luggage has

Two handcarts discovered in 2019 when clearing disused shed behind Hotspur House (John Greenwood)

proved of great advantage and we notice that some additional sidings are now being put down by Mr Kingham's workmen, which will greatly facilitate the traffic arrangements."

At this time, there not yet being a rail link to Southampton, much of the produce sold in the Hythe and district shops came across by ferry. Once unloaded, the porters would stow it onto the trolleys and push it along the pier to waiting, in the most, horse drawn vans.

THE HEARTBEAT OF HYTHE

The Hampshire Independent for June 1, 1918, reported: "A good consignment of beef for Hythe and the district was received here yesterday afternoon having been sent from Southampton by the 3 o'clock steamer." In its July 27, 1918 edition, the same newspaper commented that Hythe and district was "very well off this week in the way of butcher's meat, judging from the large quantity that was taken over per steamer from Southampton on Thursday (25th) afternoon and which occupied a considerable time in unloading, detaining the steamer quite half-an-hour".

CONCEPTION, ACQUISITION, INSTALLATION & OPERATION

Thomas Bernard Percy

On March 22, 1920, Mr Thomas Bernard Percy, director and secretary of the General Estates Company, wrote to Lt. Col. C.V.C. Hobart of the Hythe Pier and Hythe and Southampton Ferry Co. Ltd. informing him that "an opportunity has occurred to acquire Surplus Government Railway Material suitable for an Electric Railway for Hythe Pier". "Before deciding anything it is proposed to hold a Directors Meeting" he continued, suggesting "March 31 at 2 or 3 o'clock (if) convenient to the local directors".

The acquisition of the surplus government railway material was already all but a "done deal" before the meeting with Lt. Col. Hobart, Sir Robert Hobart and Mr W Cameron took place on April 1, in which each of the local directors found Mr Percy's opportunity "very interesting".

Four months earlier, on November 25, 1919, Mr Percy had written to The Controller of the Railway Material Disposal Department of the Surplus Government Property & Disposal Board at the War Office offering £600 for three Electric Tractors including an extra battery listed under "Surplus" on page 83 of a government catalogue. Capt. L.W. Bull, Assistant Controller to the Surplus Government Property & Disposal Board responded three days later, on November 28, declining the offer and informing Mr Percy that the lowest price was "£300 each or £900 for the three" to include the 48 spare cells which were "new and in perfect working order". He further invited Mr Percy to inspect the tractors that were lying at HM Munitions Factory, St Andrews Road Station, Avonmouth.

Mr Percy again wrote to the Surplus Government Property & Disposal Board on December 23, 1919, this time submitting an offer of £675 which was "the utmost the plant is worth". Capt. Bull replied on

December 30 on behalf of the Surplus Government Property & Disposal Board again stating the lowest price to be £900.

Mr Percy wrote once again on March 11, 1920 asking whether his offer of £675 would now be acceptable if the plant was still unsold; the Surplus Government Property & Disposal Board responding two days later,

Brush tractor at Gretna Munitions Factory (number unknown)

on March 13 with an offer to meet the General Estates Company "half-way" at £800. Mr Percy replied on March 16 pointing out that "half-way" should read £787 10s and should the Surplus Government Property & Disposal Board be agreeable then he had his director's instruction to accept such a figure.

Finally, agreement was reached. Mr Sidney C Sheppard on behalf of the Surplus Government Property & Disposal Board confirmed such in a letter dated March 18, 1920. He included a Tender Form to be signed and returned with cheque payment for the three tractors, numbers 16302, 16304 and 16307 lying at Avonmouth.

These four-wheeled tractor units had been built in 1917 by the Brush Electrical Engineering Co. Ltd of Loughborough for use at the Avonmouth Mustard Gas Factory where they were operated at 100 volts, from Iron-clad Exide batteries sited fore and aft of a driving cab. Each of these batteries comprised 48 cells arranged into 4 trays of 12, facilitating easy removal. The 156 amperes hours capacity of the battery enabled the tractor to cover 15 miles on one charge spread over an 8-hour day. A one-hour midday boost would add 5 miles, offering 10 miles before and 10 miles after the boost, 20 miles for the day; the battery being fully recharged overnight. At Avonmouth the tractors could haul loads of three to four tons at a speed of 5 miles per hour on the level, slower on slight gradients.

The inter-polar type of motor is a Brush standard design, wound for 80/100 volts direct current, running at 900 rpm, producing 2.75 hp. In a 1929 railway magazine article, author C. F. Klapper reveals the motor to be running satisfactorily at Hythe at 1800 rpm producing 5.5 hp, sufficient for a hauling capacity of 6 tons at 12 mph. Mr. Klapper gave the starting current as 80 amperes

Battery Loco in Working Trim as illustrated in The Locomotive publication February 1919

with a running current of 28 amperes average. The weekly current consumption was in 1929 71 KWH for 14 return journeys on weekdays and 9 on Sundays. Apart from routine maintenance the original motors operated until 2002 before receiving their first overhaul and rewinding. They are still in use more than one hundred years after installation. The shaft runs in gunmetal bearings lubricated by oil rings. The drive from the motor to the wheels is through a mild steel countershaft by means of silent chains and chain wheels (gear ratio 7 ½ - 1). The first drive is from the motor shaft to the countershaft, which is carried across the frame and runs in ball bearings. There are further chain drives from the countershaft to each axle. A metal gear case covers the drive from the motor shaft to the counter shaft. The controller gives 3 speeds in either direction. The first speed is for starting only, there being resistance in circuit with the motor. The second notch gives approximately half-speed with load torque, the third notch gives full speed with full load torque. An ironclad circuit breaker is fitted controlling the supply to the motor.

The cast steel wheels are 14" diameter on tread, the axles running in ball bearings bolted to forged stretcher bars set down at the ends to form seating for the coiled bearings springs, which are provided with guides passing through the centre. The wheelbase (track width) is 2 feet with the distance between the centres of the front and rear wheels being 3 feet; each wheel being 16" in diameter.

The hand brake is lined with "Ferodo" and acts on a cast iron drum secured to the countershaft and is operated by a hand wheel attached to a spindle screwed at the lower end to increase the braking effect.

Tractor before entering service at Hythe

From bottom of wheel to top of driving cab the tractors are 6 feet 6 inches in height, from buffer to buffer 9 feet in length and 3 feet 8 inches in width (the tractors being hand built, each is marginally different).

Mr Gerald Yorke, who had been engaged as a consultant engineer for the project, visited the Avonmouth Works on April 13, 1920, having made a visit to the Southend-on-Sea Pier Railway on April 10 for the purpose of comparison. Initial concerns over potential vibration were eased on account of this visit as the larger scale rolling stock there did not cause vibration greater than expected. Regarding his visit to Avonmouth, Mr Yorke reported that the Chief Electrical Engineer had informed him that the batteries had recently been inspected by the Chloride Battery Co, which had pronounced them to be in "excellent condition". Together, the Avonmouth Chief Engineer and Mr Yorke had further discussed the extra load the tractors would endure and agreed to their suitability for the Pier project.

Considerable discussion between Mr Yorke and Mr Percy and his staff at Hythe on the logistics and practicality of the installation of the railway system followed. At the time there was no facility at Hythe for recharging the batteries so an Aster 8kw set was identified by Mr Yorke, who was instructed by Mr Percy in a letter dated April 18 to make an offer of £150 for it. Once the equipment was procured then Mr Yorke was authorised to go ahead with securing the tractors and batteries from Avonmouth.

Mr Percy returned the Tender Form on April 22, 1920, with a request to delay the removal of the tractors from Avonmouth by no more than 70 days whilst the recharging issue was addressed. Mr Sidney C Sheppard, on behalf of the Surplus Government Property & Disposal Board, acknowledged receipt of both the tender and Mr Percy's request to delay removal of the tractors on April 30 with a date for such removal to be by June 30, 1920. Mr Percy forwarded cheques to the value of £787 10s (£424 GEC / £363 10s Hythe Pier and Hythe and Southampton Ferry Co Ltd) on May 6.

The charging equipment eventually secured was a 7kw Parsons petrol/paraffin generating set built at Parsons Southampton Works at a cost of £150. Upon confirmation of its availability Mr Percy wrote to the Surplus Government Property & Disposal Board on May 13, 1920 advising it that the charging equipment had been secured and accordingly he was able to take delivery of the tractors "almost immediately". Mr Roberts, manager at Hythe, was instructed to pay £25 to lorry owners Wimbletons for the transport of the generating equipment from Minster to Hythe. It arrived during the late afternoon of May 28, 1920.

The tractors left Avonmouth by rail on June 15, arriving at Totton Railway Station on June 19 for onward transportation by road to Hythe two days later. Although the Surplus Government Property & Disposal Board were willing to allow some lengths of track for the facility of off-loading at Hythe to be shipped at the same time and that the rails were lying available for shipping, the Superintendent at Avonmouth would not release them as he had not been officially informed to do so by the Surplus Government Property & Disposal Board. Accordingly, Mr Roberts was instructed to procure four lengths of rail locally.

The costs were escalating, as pointed out by Mr Percy in a letter to Mr Yorke dated June 7, 1920. Mr Percy added: "The ferry has not been a paying concern for many months, and it is necessary that we carefully watch every expense."

The power for the tractors (batteries removed) would be supplied from a new purpose-built generating station near the tollhouse at 200 volts DC, dropped to 100 volts by loss resistors, using a purpose designed contact shoe from a third rail. Mr Yorke submitted a plan for encasing the live rail power source in a wooden frame with a one-inch top gap for the contact shoe that "not even a child could get its foot down in it". Mr Yorke assured Mr Percy "the cost would be a great deal less than the fencing in of the track". "This plan" he continued "would give the

Installation of the tracks, shore end, 1920

full width of the pier for walking on and obviate the other disadvantages of railing off a portion".

Mr Yorke also recommended a separate power supply at a cost of approximately £80 for the pier lighting away from the railway supply to alleviate plunging the pier and its landing stages into darkness should the latter fail.

Prior to the generation station being operational, familiarisation of the controls of the tractors was perfected under battery power. In an interview in 1992 to mark his 90th birthday, Harry Banks, a retired ferry skipper recalled the tractors running by battery.

Owing to an objection from the landlord of the Drummond Arms Hotel, plans to locate the running shed across from his building were changed. Work on laying the track on the south side of the pier commenced but was constantly delayed as the wooden decking was "found out to be in a far worse condition than appeared at first glance". Mr Roberts was tasked with sourcing replacement timber, made more difficult by Mr Percy's fastidious scrutinising of costs.

Into 1921, the laying of the 2 feet gauge track continued. Flat bottom rails joined by fishplates were mounted on sleepers bolted to the pier decking. The track would run the full length of the Pier with additional sidings at the shore end. A successful trial of running two tractors in tandem was carried out on February 27, 1922.

An order was placed on October 10, 1921, with the Drewry Car

Company of London to supply two passenger carriages for the Hythe Pier Tramway. The carriages were built by Baguley Cars Ltd of Burton-on-Trent (Baguley Order No. 1463) as part of a working arrangement between the two companies. The original order would be amended several times, in the main regarding the draw gear. The final invoice price would be £375 each.

Each of the first two carriages rode on two four-wheeled bogies, designed to be able pass round a curve of 19 feet 6 inches to get into a shed. Between centres, the distance between the fore and aft wheels is 3 feet 6 inches; each wheel being sized as per the tractors. The carriages were 16 feet long, 7 feet 6 inches high and 4 feet 9 inches wide, fitted with slatted wooden seating and able to carry 18-20 passengers. The body of the carriage was framed in teak, coated with "Pegamoid" (a former trade name of a waterproof varnish). Access to the carriages was through sliding doors on the north side only, although the original drawings show the carriages to have standard opening doors with windows that lowered to gain access to the door opening mechanism on the outside of the carriage. Windows were fixed throughout the carriage on the finished product. Electric lighting was to be supplied via cables running outside along the roof of the carriages from the driving tractor.

The first of the carriages, Drewry Trailer Car number 1047 was dispatched on May 26, 1922, followed by the second, Drewry Trailer

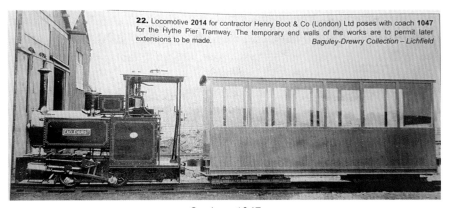

22. Locomotive **2014** for contractor Henry Boot & Co (London) Ltd poses with coach **1047** for the Hythe Pier Tramway. The temporary end walls of the works are to permit later extensions to be made.   *Baguley-Drewry Collection – Lichfield*

Carriage 1047

Car number 1048 on June 22. After trial runs along the Pier the Hythe Pier Railway was ready to roll. Without ceremony the first passenger run took place during late July 1922 (no record of the exact date can be traced). The early layout of the rake was

Carriages 1047 and 1048, 1922

a tractor at each end with the two carriages between.

The railway was an immediate success but there were problems, highlighting additional rolling stock would be needed. Ferry passengers would often have to walk the pier (or wait for a second train from the shore end) owing to the number of people using the train to get to the pier head to fish, to bathe, use the yacht club or simply joyride. Getting the train away also often took a considerable time owing to the conductor selling tickets and giving change.

An order for two more carriages was placed with the Drewry Car Company on March 10, 1923 at a cost of £340 each. These, however, were driving carriages, slightly longer at 16 feet 2 inches, slightly shorter at 7 feet 1 inch and 5 feet wide, with the same slatted wooden seating able to carry 16-18 passengers. The driving carriages would have controls at their seaward ends identical to those of the tractors and like the ordinary carriages be equipped with a central buffer and couplings at both ends. Once in service the layout of the rake would become a driving carriage at the seaward end with the two ordinary carriages between it and a tractor at the shore end. The second driving carriage would be held in spare along with the second and third tractors although it would occasionally be pressed into service as a temporary replacement for an ordinary carriage when one was withdrawn for maintenance.

Mr Percy demanded delivery of at least one of the second order of carriages be in time for the Whitsun Holiday on May 21, 1923. Drewry

Car number 1327 was dispatched on May 12 whilst Drewry Car number 1328 followed two days later.

For expediency Mr Percy decreed that the final inspection would be undertaken by Mr Yorke on arrival at Hythe. Mr Yorke reported back to Mr Percy that the first of the new carriages "was in

Early image of the train, circa 1920s

such a disgracefully defective condition (it) was not able to take to the run even as a trailer". Mr Yorke added that he had "interviewed the Managing Director of the Car Co and expressed (himself) very strongly on the subject". The constructors had agreed to send engineers to Hythe to rectify the issues which included among a catalogue of faults, "unsatisfactory brakes".

On July 28, 1923, an extremely disappointed Mr Percy wrote to the Drewry Car Co: "These two cars were ordered on the understanding that they would be delivered 2 clear weeks before Whit Monday viz May 7th and they were actually paid for on May 10th. All the time since, they have been unusable, and we are now approaching the August Bank Holiday. Will you please use every endeavour to enable us to use these cars during the Holiday, otherwise a whole season will have passed with this Company housing two useless cars." No record can be traced as to whether this was done.

Two four-wheeled luggage trucks originally used on the tracks laid down by Mr Kingham in 1909 were modified for use on the Hythe Pier Railway. These were 7 feet 6 inches long x 3 feet 6 inches wide and have been used to carry all manner of items along the track. Simply, if it fitted and the driver could still see, then it would be carried.

Next to the tollhouse, offices were built for the Hythe Electricity Company set up to supply the pier, the sheds, and the railway. As the capacity generated by the new generating station behind the offices far exceeded requirements, the General Estates

Generating plant (General Estates/Hythe Electricity) in Hythe workshop, circa 1926

Company, owners of the Hythe Electricity Company, took the decision to sell the surplus power. It was not long before much of the village was connected to a DC supply through a system of poles and wires.

During 1930, the West Hampshire Electricity Company made an offer of £6,000 for Mr Percy's power generation business that was deemed inadequate and accordingly refused. By the beginning of 1931, however, Mr Percy was proposing selling the business but the offer from the West Hampshire Electricity Company was revised to £5,000. Mr Yorke, who had been retained as a consultant engineer (at a remuneration of £20 p.a. for services in regard to the Hythe Pier Railway and £40 for those afforded the electricity undertaking), advised Mr Percy in January 1931 that the approach to the West Hampshire Electricity Company was "badly timed with the market so depressed in every direction". However, negotiations continued with contracts being exchanged late in August and the business transferred on September 11, 1931. The Hythe Electricity Company continued to supply the West Hampshire Electricity Company until the latter had converted the Hythe system from direct to alternating current. Supply ceased on December 19, 1931.

Power to the Hythe Pier and its Railway continued to be supplied from the company's own generating plant but during 1932 consideration was given to saving costs by taking the power supply for all its requirements from the West Hampshire Electricity Company. This would entail using alternating current rather than the direct current generated by its own plant. Converting the tractor motors to alternating current also had to be considered. Gerald Yorke recommended the lighting on the pier and its office and ancillary buildings should be converted to alternating current in his quarterly report in April 1932 but added that a rectifier should be installed in the running shed for the train driver to switch on when direct current for the train was required.

Mr Roberts, manager of the Hythe Pier, Train and Ferry, had written to Mr Percy strongly urging him to resist converting the tractor motors on February 8, 1932, and not to take supply from the West Hampshire Electricity Co, which had "failed several times since they took it over from us". "Our Pier Railway is our greatest asset," he continued. "If we had no means of transport on the Pier our passenger traffic would decrease considerably, passengers would not walk in wet or cold weather but would travel by bus." Mr Roberts ramped up his argument by adding: "The train induces a lot of passengers to travel by ferry who would otherwise go by bus."

Mr Roberts would remind Mr Percy of his reservations many times over the following twelve months but by April 1933 negotiations to take the power supply from the West Hampshire Electricity Co were in an advanced stage. In a letter dated April 10, 1933, Mr Roberts urged Mr Percy during these negotiations not to overlook "the probability of the failure of their supply which has failed on numerous occasions and the serious consequences it would have on the ferry". Mr Percy responded in a letter dated April 11, 1933: "No system of travel is exempt from failure. If the current fails for a couple of hours at Hythe, the passengers will walk, as they did regularly for many years previous to the provision of a tramway."

On the same day Mr Percy wrote to the Hewettic Electric Co Ltd of Walton-on-Thames for information about a rectifier suitable for operating the Pier Railway.

By August 25, 1933, the decision to take power from the West Hampshire Electricity Co was confirmed. A specification for the rectifier converter set to supply the Hythe Pier Railway (as follows) was forwarded to the Hewettic Electric Company.

INCOMING SUPPLY PRESSURE	400 volts, three phase, 50 cycles, earthed neutral.
OUTPUT PRESSURE	210 volts, D.C. earthed negative.
RATED OUTPUT	15 KW continuous. Train starting current 80-90 amperes, decreasing to steady load of 30-35 amperes within 15 seconds; only one train in operation. Train journey occupies 2 minutes followed by a wait of approximately 5 minutes for return journey. Normal running 2 complete trips up and down for each hourly boat. Bank holidays boats run half-hourly. Other load to be supplied 1.5 H.P. motor in repair shop.
TRANSFORMER	To comply with B.S. specification 171 of 1927. Tappings on primary plus and minus 2 ½% and 5%. Alternative quotations for inclusion of air and oil immersed types to be rendered. (As installation site is on the waterside and exposed to damp sea air, it may be considered preferable to employ the oil immersed type).
RECTIFIER	The smoothing devices to be of such efficiency that no interference is caused to any telephone telegraph or wireless receiving circuits in the vicinity.

The voltage rise or light load to be so limited that the train lighting current amounting to 1 ½ amperes shall be sufficient to keep such rises within the limits which the lamps will sustain without damage or undue shortening of their life.

The unit to be fitted with main triple pole, ironclad switch, and fuses (combined unit) on the A.C. side of ample capacity, i.e., 50 or 60 amperes size. On the D.C. side the unit will feed direct on to existing D.C. switchboard panel, so that switchgear or instruments will be required on the output side.

Remote controlled triple pole contactor switch to be fitted on the A.C. side for remote push button control, so that train drivers may switch off unit in between trips, unless workshop motor is required in service.

Customer will run necessary leads from this switch to the control point.

The Hewettic Electric Company quoted for the manufacture and supply on September 2, 1933, complete with a fully enclosed sheet metal cabinet (30" x 36" x 66" high") with front fully accessible access doors, the sum of £120. After obtaining and subsequently rejecting alternate quotations an order was placed with Hewettic Electric on October 19 with one or two minor adjustments to the specification. The rectifier was delivered to Hythe on December 12 and subsequently installed. With Mr Yorke in attendance, it was successfully started up on December 22, 1933.

In the meantime, the General Estates Company had advertised the shortly to be redundant generating plant for sale in assorted trade journals at an ambitious price of £1,250. As little interest was forthcoming, Mr Percy agreed Mr Roberts' more realistic

ONE Twin-cyl. VICKERS-PETTERS SEMI-DIESEL ENGINE, 60-66-h.p., direct coupled to Metropolitan-Vickers Dynamo, shunt wound, 39-kw., 186 amps., 210 volts, 325 r.p.m., D.C., with switchboard panel, circuit breaker, switches and instruments complete. One Single-cyl. ROBEY SEMI-DIESEL ENGINE, 35-h.p., coupled to E.C.C. Dynamo, 20-kw., 91 amps., 220 volts, 275 r.p.m., D.C., with switchboard panel, circuit breaker, switches and instruments complete One BATTERY CHARGING BOOSTER, giving 32 volts at 35 amps., or 80 volts at 11 amps., 1,450 r.p.m., D.C., with switchboard panels, circuit breaker, switches and instruments complete. One BATTERY CHARGING BOOSTER, giving 35 volts at 45 amps., or 80 volts at 19 amps., 1,450 r.p.m., D.C., with switchboard panels, circuit breaker, switches and instruments complete. One BATTERY of ACCUMULATORS, 119 cells, 240 amp.-hour capacity. One BATTERY of ACCUMULATORS, 113 cells, 160 amp.-hour capacity. Price £1,250. Apply G.E. CO., LTD., 20, BOND STREET, EALING, LONDON, W. 5. 2-7193414

GEC advertisement for redundant generating plant, October 1933

valuation of £450 (or best offer). The equipment was sold to a Mr. Phillips of Chesham at the beginning of November 1933 for the sum of £362 10s. However, before completion of this sale Mr Phillips' Principle was killed in a railway accident putting it on hold pending an inquest. During this time Mr Percy accepted an offer of £400 from a Mr Charles Jones of Stoke on Trent.

Electricity supply for the train, the pier and the Hythe offices proceeded to be taken from the West Hampshire Electricity Company, resulting in the redundancy of the Hythe Electricity Company and its staff including Mr Oswald Philip, clerk, and manager.

The advent of war just five years later necessitated the acquisition of replacement back-up generating equipment. This survived in a separate building just outside of where the pier gates are today until 2014.

During the early 1930s the Hythe Pier Railway proved to be the jewel in the crown of Mr Percy's Hythe Ferry business. However, it was a business that was struggling against competition from the Fawley – Totton Branch Railway Line and much improved omnibus services.

Hythe Pier train, early 1930s

Running repairs were being found to be needed more frequently. Mr Yorke was making quarterly visits to Hythe and reporting back to Mr Percy. His reports, more often than not, included detail of necessary maintenance to the railway track, the tractors and rolling stock, all with financial implications. On July 29, 1932, Mr Percy accepted a quotation of £19 12s 0d from the Drewry Car Company for two pairs of cast steel wheels for one of the tractors. These were sub-contracted via the Baguley Car Company to Hadfields Ltd of Sheffield and dispatched via Baguley on November 17, 1932, for collection from Hythe Railway Station. (Each wheel is recorded as weighing 47 lbs). Delivery of the wheels would allow for the re-introduction into service of the third tractor, side-lined for a little while. Two sets of wheels complete with axles for the control department end of one of the driving carriages were ordered from the Drewry Car Company on January 30, 1933, at £24 for the pair.

Despite his protestations, Mr Roberts cut wages of some staff (including that of his own son) by 10 shillings per week but still Mr Percy demanded cost reductions suggesting that perhaps the pierman could also act as conductor on the train or maybe the conductor also as pierman. The train, he pointed out, was making two return journeys per hour with the conductor's wages absorbing the receipts. In a letter on March 15, 1933, Mr Percy indicated to Mr Roberts he was paying too much in wages and it was clear that the time had come for drastic changes. In an earlier letter to Mr Roberts dated March 3, 1933, Mr Percy wrote that the Hythe Ferry was "hardly worth while continuing".

Mr Yorke was invited to find cost savings but reported back that further wheel replacements were required on both the other driving carriage and the tractors. Mr Yorke added in his report of March 22, 1933: "The Railway has been in operation for ten years, and the maintenance has remained very low, during that period, it is to be expected that a certain amount of renewals will have to be made." He continued: "In former reports (first mooted in October 1931), the advisability of purchasing some motor coaches to replace the tractors has been mentioned, as the weight per axle could thus be substantially reduced, and consequently likewise the wear and tear on the Pier structure." He concluded: "In view of the general financial stringency, that your company will rather defer consideration of such expenditure to a later period."

Mr Yorke revived his position on upgrading the Hythe Pier Railway in 1935. In his report, dated August 8, he informed Mr Percy that one tractor (16304) "was now permanently out of commission, some of its parts having been used to maintain the other two in service; and these latter are in none too good a condition". He further argued that it would not be prudent to spend more on re-conditioning them, favouring procurement of two new motor coaches.

In his report of December 22, 1935, Mr Yorke informed Mr Percy that quotations were in hand for a new motor coach which should be procured and once tested and found satisfactory the decision could be taken to order a second "so that the tractors could be scrapped and simultaneously work could be commenced to alter gradually the old stock to match in with the new".

At this time, it became essential to replace the 41-year-old paddle ferry **Hampton**. Not only did this consume Mr Percy's time, but it also involved great expense. As the new ferryboat was designed and subsequently built, the Hythe Pier Railway continued to work tirelessly, making light of Mr Yorke's reservations. By the time the new boat, the **Hotspur II**, started to ply the waters between Hythe and Southampton, replacement of the tractors with new rolling stock appears to have been consigned to history.

THE HEARTBEAT OF HYTHE

HOW TO DRIVE THE TRAIN

TRACTOR 14302 CONTROL CAB

1 Spotlight Switch
2 Power Supply Breaker
3 Front Windscreen
4 Solenoid Housing
5 Carriages' Light Switch
6 Pier CCTV Sign
7 Deadman's Handle

8 Contactor Housing
9 Nut/Bolt Fixing
10 Brake Wheel Handle
11 Brake Wheel
12 Hinged Seat
13 Cable Speed Selector
   – Tractor Motor

14 Speed Selector Lever
   (which also selects
   direction, two small
   brass plates indicate
   Hythe or Southampton)
15 Speed Selector Housing
16 DC Tractor Motor

TRAINING LOG/METHOD STATEMENT
Train Operating Procedure
(Reproduced courtesy Blue Funnel Ferries)

	Tick when undertaken
Preliminary:	
1 Know where the isolation switch is located.	
2 Know where the emergency switch is located.	
Object:	
To transport passengers to and from both ends of the pier in total safety.	
NOTE: The train carriages are seating only. **No standing is permitted.** Maximum capacity however will vary.	
1 From Hythe end, release brake in tractor unit.	
2 Check selector is in neutral.	
3 Check selector is in neutral in drive coach end.	
4 Push and release Deadman to double check both ends are out of gear.	
5 Check mirror to make sure all is clear on station to move off.	
6 Select first gear, **(do not use 2nd gear when leaving station)** check mirrors, depress Deadman handle.	
7 Travel **slowly** at least full length of train to lamppost 3. Keep constant lookout in mirror for passengers running to train and stop if necessary.	
8 Then change into second gear.	
9 Continue at a moderate, safe speed; use the brake to control speed if the wind starts to push train too quickly. **SPEED** Brisk walk/slow jog. No faster. Use only third gear when extreme weather conditions dictate. In normal conditions **DO NOT** use third gear.	
10 At midway point, take up any slack in the brake.	
11 At approximately lamppost 22/23 ease down by slowly applying brake.	
12 **Make sure gear is in neutral on final braking.**	
13 By lamppost 26 the train should be at a medium walking pace – **no quicker.**	
14 Enter station at a slow walking pace. Brake continually – do not leave to the last few metres.	

15 At pier end station wait at top of passenger brow especially at busy times, to look down ramp to ensure slow/elderly passengers are not left coming up ramp and if the train is full ask others to wait in waiting room and offer to run a second train.	
16 **Drive coaches only – Emergency braking aid.** In event of **extreme emergency only** additional braking force can be applied by pressing **left** foot on brake chain carefully at bottom braking column. **An incident report form must be completed if this action is taken.**	

Returning:	
1 Re-check gear is in neutral; handbrake off.	

Return to Hythe:	
1 Check Deadman to make sure both ends are out of gear.	
2 Select first gear, check mirror to see if all clear before moving off.	
3 Select second gear after moving length of train.	
4 Maintain a moderate safe speed.	
5 Take up any slack in brake.	
6 Use the brake to prevent wind driving train too quickly.	
7 At lamppost 6 down to medium walking pace.	
8 Select neutral and glide down into station at a slow walking speed.	
9 Apply brake constantly to avoid braking too hard for the last few yards.	

Bowser:	
Only push/pull bowser using first gear. Only use second gear if the weather is against you.	

Weather conditions:	
Note: Strong **wind** and rain do have an influence on the train, do not allow them to push the train too quickly.	
The worst conditions for braking at Hythe end are when a sea mist is present; this creates a greasy track; **extreme care must be used and an even slower approach is necessary.**	

Instructor's Name:

Instructor's Signature:

_____

_____

Trainee's Name:

Trainee's Signature:

_____

_____

Date: _____

Time: _____

LIVE RAIL ISOLATION PROCEDURE

Third Rail Isolation (Safe working practice)		
1	When requested by personnel to isolate the third rail, turn the isolation switch in the box to the **OFF** position, the red light on top of the box should go off indicating that the power is no longer on, tell the person who requested the isolation that the power is now off.	
2	Take the Red Lock and Key from the box, close the box door and lock with the Red Lock, the Key should either be put in your pocket or handed to the person who is working on the track.	
3	**The track must not be turned back on until the person who requested its isolation asks for it to be turned back on.**	
4	Once the correct request has been received unlock the box. Before turning power on call on the radio that the power is coming back on, **GET A CONFIRMATION,** only when you are sure everybody is clear of the track turn the isolation switch to the **ON** position, the red light on top of the box should come on. Call on the radio that the power is now back on.	
5	Hang Red Lock and Key on the hook inside the isolation box and close the box as normal.	

YOU'VE HAD THE TUITION, NOW TAKE THE TEST...

You may need to take a stroll down the pier
with your eyes open first! Ask questions too!
Answers on page 86

TRAIN DRIVER KNOWLEDGE TEST

(Reproduced courtesy Blue Funnel Ferries)

Driver's Name		Date of Test	
Paper marked by		Score	
Driver trained by			

Instructions for candidate
Please place a tick in the box next to your chosen answer

1	**What is the first thing you do to get a train moving from Hythe?**	
a	Depress the Deadman Handle	
b	Disengage any safety devices	
c	Disengage the brake wheel	
2	**Before starting to move the train, what is the main passenger safety check you make?**	
a	Everyone has a valid ticket	
b	Passengers are all seated, doors are closed	
c	Check your mirror	
3	**What is meant by the term "Arcing"?**	
a	The distance between the train and the platform	
b	The distance between cars on a three-car train	
c	A luminous bridge formed in a gap between two electrodes	
4	**When should the brakes be applied before arriving at a station?**	
a	Well ahead of stopping point	
b	After the train has coasted to a standstill	
c	Gradually using brake point markers	
5	**What happens when you remove your hand from the Deadman's Handle?**	
a	The solenoid is deactivated and power to the motor is cut	
b	The motor goes into neutral	
c	Nothing	

6	Where would you find the main drive sprocket?				
a	Drive coach				
b	Passenger coach				
c	Tractor unit				
7	You're attempting to depart Pierhead & Deadman does not engage the solenoid & the train will not move. What is the first item to check?				
a	Is the shoe in contact with the live rail				
b	Are the train lights on				
c	Is the brake still on				
8	How do you disengage the Brake Wheel lock?				
a	Turn the Brake Wheel slightly clockwise				
b	Turn the Brake Wheel slightly anti-clockwise				
c	Move the Selector Handle to the first position to disengage the Brake Wheel				
9	Where would you find the oiler?				
a	Driver coach				
b	Passenger coach				
c	Tractor unit				
10	How many blue diodes should be in the draw?	10	20	30	None
11	What size are the nuts for the transformer fuses?	10mm	20mm	5mm	6mm
12	What amperage are the transformer fuses?	50amp	60amp	70amp	100amp
13	What should you do if you think there is a fault on the train?				
a	Report fault by paperwork system				
b	Report fault by paperwork system and contact an engineer and seek advice				
c	Drive the train very slowly				
14	When engineers are working on the train whilst in service in the station,what should the driver always do?				
a	Make the tea				
b	Sweep the station				
c	Ensure the trackside power is switched off				

15	Fuel tank readings are kept for?	
a	So the train driver knows what is in the tank	
b	For the Inland Revenue purposes	
c	For both of the above	
d	For no real reason at all	
e	Accounts at Head Office	
16	Whilst the train is in motion, what should the amp gauge in the workshop read?	
a	0-45 and drops down to 10 amps	
b	74	
c	240	
17	How many lampposts along the pier?	
a	26	
b	22	
c	20	
d	Other	

THE HEARTBEAT OF HYTHE

GERALD YORKE

Gerald Yorke was born on March 1, 1884, at 7 Eldon Road, Kensington, London, at the home of his grandparents, Samuel and Emily Peeke. His baptism record shows him as being the son of Richard Frederick and Elizabeth Katherine Yorke of 102, Sinclair Road, West Kensington, London, who subsequently produced Gerald a brother and a sister. Gerald Yorke resided with his grandparents for the greater part of his first twenty years. He suffered much ill-health, all the childhood ailments and a rheumatic fever.

Gerald Yorke, circa 1920

At an early age he was sent to St. Pauls Preparatory School, where he was to win one of twelve scholarships which entitled him to a silver fish to be worn on his watch chain. He joined the Officers Training Corps as a cadet. He would have liked to have joined the Army but at that time an officer needed a private income, beyond the means of his recently retired grandfather.

He matriculated from school at the age of sixteen and was apprenticed to Cammel Laird at its shipbuilding yard in Birkenhead. Whilst there, he was injured during an incident and just two years into his apprenticeship returned to London to enrol into the South Western Polytechnic Engineering College. In 1904, at the age of twenty, he joined the Central London Railway Company.

The Central London Railway Company had been formed in 1889 and was taken over by the Underground Electric Railways Company of London (UERL) in 1913. Its assets were absorbed into the London Passenger Transport Board (LPTB), a public owned corporation, on July 1, 1933, along with those of the UERL, the Metropolitan Railway (MR) and all bus and tram operators within the London Passenger Transport Area (LPTA).

On March 8, 1904, Gerald Yorke married Emily Harriet Butler, setting up home in Little Ealing Lane, London. The 1911 census shows Gerald Yorke and his wife living at 8, Airedale Road, Ealing, with two daughters, Ivy Violet and Esme. Two more children – another daughter, Gladys, and a son, Percy Oliver (Bill in later life) – followed.

In 1915, Gerald Yorke answered Lord Kitchener's call to arms. His failure to reveal to the recruiting officer that he was not only a married man with four children but also employed in a reserved occupation saw him assigned to the Royal Engineers, in which his highest rank achieved was corporal. He served in France before being sent to Mesopotamia, corresponding these days to most of Iraq and eastern Syria. There, he met a man called Bill Cooper, who was to become a great friend long after the war. He was demobbed in 1919 but suffered considerable ill-health during the immediate ensuing years.

He returned to his employment with the railway company and in 1920 he was asked by an associate, Thomas Bernard Percy, to assist with the planning and installation of the Hythe Pier Railway. Once this was complete, he was retained as a consultant engineer to the General Estates Company, proprietors of the Hythe Ferry and owners of the Hythe Pier and Railway, well into the 1940s. He was a regular visitor to Hythe right up until his retirement, staying at first with friends and subsequently at the Drummond Arms Hotel, opposite the pier.

In addition to his involvement with the Hythe project, he and a friend had a "side-line" filling batteries in a workshop he had built in the garden of his home at 8, Airedale Road. It was at this time his marriage failed and his wife, Emily, left, leaving him to bring up his four children, a difficult task at a time when he was also studying for AMIE certification (Associate Member of the Institution of Engineers). In 1925, he filed for divorce with the dissolution of the marriage being finalised in February 1926.

Gerald Yorke 1951

Whilst the divorce proceedings were taking their course, Gerald Yorke took a break, staying at a boarding house close by his wartime friend Bill Cooper in the Devon resort of Paignton. Whilst there, he met Phyllis Hodges and a courtship developed, leading to marriage in October 1926. The new Mrs Yorke left her home in Bristol and moved in with her new husband and his four children at 8, Airedale Road. This arrangement proved to be difficult and consequently the three daughters, all by this time working, moved out. Percy Oliver, the youngest and still at school, stayed on. Phyllis produced Gerald another daughter, Sheila, on January 24, 1929.

During the General Strike of 1926, Gerald Yorke, along with a team of navy stokers, was confined in a power station at Lots Road, Chelsea, to ensure the electrical supply to the London Underground was maintained. A permanent guard was posted outside the facility. Into the 1930s Gerald Yorke was busily employed by the newly formed LPTB, travelling all over the London Underground network, working on new line extensions, new stations, and power supply facilities. It is a wonder he found time for his consultancy work at Hythe.

In 1937, the Yorkes moved to 247 Malden Road, Cheam, a large, detached house with an extensive garden. It would seem Gerald Yorke over-stretched his budget for the family always struggled financially. Despite this, they took advantage of employee passes allowing cheap travel by train and bus enabling annual trips to Devon and to see Phyllis's family in Bristol. In August 1939, with the country on the brink of war, Gerald Yorke enjoyed his last holiday for six years in Swanage, Dorset.

The Yorkes' home at 247 Malden Road was outside the London evacuation area, so the family remained together. Bombs occasionally fell nearby, as did a V1 "doodlebug" exploding opposite causing extensive damage to the property. Gerald Yorke worked such irregular

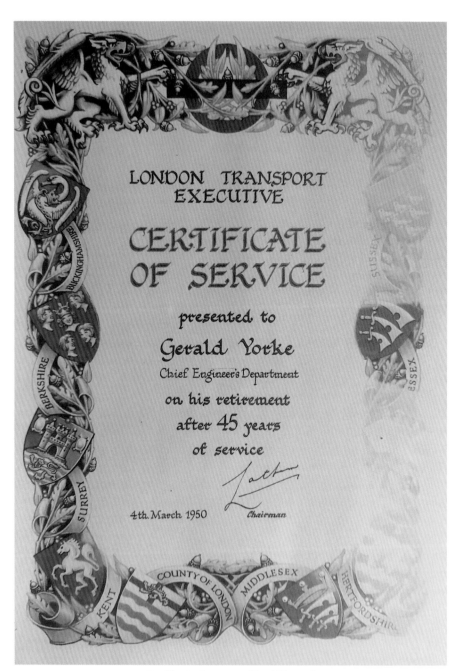

LONDON TRANSPORT
EXECUTIVE

CERTIFICATE
OF SERVICE

presented to

Gerald Yorke

Chief Engineer's Department

on his retirement

after 45 years

of service

4th March 1950   *Chairman*

Certificate (courtesy Nigel Hasted)

hours throughout the conflict, he was unable to participate in Civil Defence work or join the Home Guard. However, he did get involved in fire-watching during the final months of the war.

Gerald Yorke retirement presentation, February 20, 1950 (courtesy Nigel Hasted)

Gerald Yorke retired in 1950 and soon afterwards was diagnosed with Parkinson's Disease. Despite this debilitation he managed to escort his youngest daughter down the aisle in 1951. Already a grandfather to Esme's daughter Jennifer, by this time 15, his youngest daughter produced him a second granddaughter, Sara, in 1952. The grandson he craved duly arrived when Nigel was born in November 1955.

Gerald York's health deteriorated during the mid-late 1950s and he passed away at his Malden Road home in May 1958.

Gerald Yorke is commemorated on a plank close by the pier head station. In May 2021, the Hythe Pier Heritage Association further acknowledged his contribution to the story of the Hythe Pier Railway in naming tractor 16307 "Gerald Yorke".

Gerald Yorke plank (John Greenwood)

THE HEARTBEAT OF HYTHE

FIT FOR A KING

Shortly before D Day in 1944, the Hythe – Southampton Ferry was approached by the authorities to secretly land HRH King George VI on Hythe Pier during a visit to inspect the many craft assembled in preparation for the invasion of Europe on June 6. Mr William Arthur Lane, acting manager, was heavily involved with local organisation, under the utmost secrecy.

Whilst researching for my first book about the Hythe Pier and Ferry during the early 1970s, I received the letters (reproduced below) from Commander John W. Rayner R.N, detailing the event.

15TH SEPTEMBER, 1973

Dear Mr Titheridge,

With reference to your letter in last night's Echo, have you got the story of his late Majesty King George VI riding on the train the length of Hythe Pier following a visit to Southampton just prior to D Day in 1944?

I had the honour of receiving him at the seaward end of the pier and riding in the train with him.

If you already have the story please do not trouble to reply to this note but if you want any further information I shall be only too pleased to supply it.

Yours sincerely

John W. Rayner Commander R.N.

19TH SEPTEMBER, 1973

Dear Mr Titheridge,

Thank you for your letter of the 17th.

The enclosed is somewhat lengthy and so please hack it to pieces as so you wish. I shall not have the slightest objection.

Yours sincerely

John W. Rayner Commander R.N.

The attachment read as follows:

HMS Squid was the shore-based Combined Operations Base at Southampton which was responsible for the administration and housing of many of the Assault Squadrons in preparation for D-Day in 1944.

It was under the command of the late Captain James with myself in second-in-command.

Hythe was included in our administration area where there was a smaller Base – HMS Squid II.

As D-Day approached Captain James and myself were informed in the utmost secrecy that H.M. King George VI was shortly going to visit the Landing Craft based in Southampton Docks and in the late afternoon of the same day would be proceeding by water to Hythe Pier and then on to Broadlands at Romsey by motor car.

The whole of this visit was "Top Secret" and the instructions were that the Hythe Pier train would carry out its normal journeys with its normal load of passengers bound for the ferry until the arrival of His Majesty.

Two parties of seamen were detailed for a "special job". The larger party were in their No. 1 dress and were kept out of sight at the landward end of the pier and about a dozen seamen in overalls and armed with brooms, brushes, mops and pails of water were hidden away in a hut at the seaward end of the pier.

About 17.00 the train arrived at the pierhead and disgorged its passage passengers onto the waiting ferry.

As soon as the last passenger was out of sight the "working party" emerged from their hut and "spring-cleaned" the train from for'ard to aft in about 8 minutes flat and then disappeared into their hut.

King George VI

In the meantime the second party of seamen had marched down the pier and taken up guard duties at each lamppost on the pier.

His Majesty arrived dead on time and I had the honour of receiving him and escorting him and his retinue onto the train and we all rode down the pier together – His Majesty receiving a salute from every rating manning the pier.

On arriving at Hythe His Majesty was received by Captain James and went and spoke to the train driver – Mr L. Pearce, who still lives in Dibden Purlieu – for a few minutes and then entered his car and left for Broadlands.

(There was always a story – probably apocryphal – that shortly before the arrival of His Majesty at Hythe, the senior police officer on duty split the seat of his best trousers and had to disappear hurriedly from sight and so missed the whole of the proceedings!)

George VI one penny coin mounted in carriage number 2 in 2018 (Alan Titheridge)

The carriage in which the King travelled was subsequently marked with a badge on a wooden mount, made by Dibden Purlieu wood sculptor Ron Lane, who was the son

William Arthur Lane (Courtesy Heather Aitken)

of William Arthur Lane. The badge was later removed by an anonymous and unscrupulous souvenir hunter. In 2018 a contemporary old one penny coin was placed into the original mount and fixed onto the actual seat in carriage number 2 upon which His Majesty sat. Attached to the adjacent carriage bodywork is a transcript from a Diary page of King George VI dated Wednesday May 24th 1944 (published by www.newforestww2.org with the permission of Her Majesty Queen Elizabeth II).

WEDNESDAY MAY 24TH

I motored to Exbury which is now a naval shore base, HMS "Masterdon", where landing craft crew are trained. I spent the day with the Eastern Task Force to see the officers & men of the British Naval Assault Force in Overlord. I was met by Sir B. Ramsay, Allied Naval Comdr. Expdy. Force, R. Ad. Sir P. Vian, Naval Comdr. Eastern Task Force & others. We went by barge, the Royal Yacht barge, down the Beaulieu River out into the Solent passing landing craft. I went on board the "Bulolo" Cmd Ship Force "G" Comdr. Douglas-Pennant, the "Largs" Comdr. Ship Force "S". R Ad. A.G. Talbot & I saw Force"J" ashore at the R.Y. Sqn. Cowes, Comdr. Oliver. From here I saw all the landing craft in Portsmouth Harbour & lunched on board the cruiser "Scylla", R. Ad. Vian's flagship. I went in a naval Rescue Motor Launch to Southampton Water & the Hamble River past all the landing craft there. I must have seen over 300 L.Cs & other ships attached in the command. I spent a most interesting day. I got back to Wilton at 6.30 pm.

Local woman Una Martin of Frost Lane Farm, Hythe wrote of hearing of the King's visit in her diary on Wednesday May 24, 1944.
"Went to Southampton market, came home on the 3.30 p.m. ferry. Heard this evening that the King came to Hythe on the 5.30 p.m. ferry. Wish I'd waited for that one."

(His Majesty actually arrived at Hythe by means of a launch.)

THE HEARTBEAT OF HYTHE

THRILLS & SPILLS

In a radio talk on the BBC West of England Home Service Children's Hour on February 12, 1952, local resident Winifred Henson Towning spoke of her regular ferry journeys between Hythe and Southampton.

"Our pier is long and thin and very business-like. Since its aim in life is simply to reach the deep water where the ferry can tie up, it does just that, scorning any clutter of amusement arcades and such. But it has something much more interesting – it has a miniature electric train which takes you from one end of the pier to the other for the modest charge of one penny. And what value for that penny! There's the little train, at the village end of the pier, standing by its little platform with all the dignity of a full-size model. It consists of two or three small wooden coaches, divided into compartments, and an electric engine at each end."

She continued: "When the driver's been for the tickets he switches on the motor and away you go, rattling along the pier with the most exciting sensations. Instead of running over more land like most trains, this one's running over the sea, and out of one window you look straight down into the slapping waves with the seagulls and the little boats bobbing up and down. Out of the other one you see the pier shelters flying past like local stations on an express run."

She concludes: "After a few minutes the train slows down, the pier stops shuddering, and you can hear yourself speak again, and everybody piles out and troops down the gangway to the ferry."

This is how the Hythe Pier Railway had been for thirty years and has been pretty much so for a further seven decades. It has been a feature of the way of life in Hythe for almost a century, trundling up and down the pier perhaps fifty or more times daily to the same beat. It has not been a humdrum life, however. Our quirky little green train has had its moments.

Despite its renowned reliability – it made a newspaper appearance for running throughout a national rail strike in October 1962 – the train has, over the years, found itself in difficulty on more than a few occasions.

The Hythe Pier Railway operated throughout a national rail strike in October 1962

At just after 9.20pm on September 13, 1962, with twenty passengers on board, it jumped the rails just as it was pulling into the shore end station. A criminal investigation was opened as a company fitter, Mr J.C. Nixon, called from his home following the incident, found a wooden wedge under the wheels of the tractor, almost certainly the cause of the derailment.

The driver, Mr Thomas Phillips, explained the incident: "I was actually braking to come into the platform and the tractor jumped into the air, shot across the lines and steeplechased along the tarmac at the side. I had a few bruises and the driver's seat is a hard one and it is not meant for steeplechasing."

He continued: "As a result of the accident, the live rail was short-circuited, and all the lights went out in the train. There was no panic among the passengers and I think they were more amazed than anything else when the train suddenly stopped, and the lights went out. People came dashing out from outside the pier to see what had happened."

Mr Nixon said: "We got the train back on the lines but found the electrical pick-up gear was damaged, so the service was out of action for the rest of the night."

The local police were informed of the finding of the wedge the following morning. Subsequent enquiries failed to find the culprit who had deliberately

The Hythe Pier train at the shore end station 1978 (Pat Waterman)

placed it on the line after the train had departed for the pierhead to collect ferry passengers just ten minutes or so beforehand. The incident was put down to mindless hooliganism.

On a cold blustery day, October 16, 1973, the train was put out of action for about a half-hour after skidding on the wet track and colliding with a temporary buffer. As part of the track at the seaward end of the pier was being worked upon the buffer was placed further along the line. There were no reports of injuries, but early commuters were caused to brave the wind and rain.

Commuters and other passengers were consigned to walking the pier on October 24, 1975, as the train was out of commission with a rectifier failure. Further mechanical problems put paid to the evening service after 6pm on March 8, 1976. A points failure at the shore end of the track caused the train to spectacularly jack-knife when approaching the sheds, resulting in damage to both track and coach bogies on April 7, 1976. The train had been along the pier, without passengers, to deliver the fuel bowser. Subsequent passengers were inconvenienced however, as the accident put the train out of commission for several hours.

In a newspaper interview in August 1977, retired train driver Roy Davis spoke of an undated incident when although applying the brake the train failed to stop and hit the buffers at the shore end. The passenger capacity was 48 but there were more than eighty, predominantly football supporters on their way home on a Saturday afternoon, "packed in like sardines".

More recently, in December 2009, during a repositioning of rolling

What not to do when switching points (Sath Naidoo)

stock, the tractor and a carriage derailed whilst navigating the points at the shore-end station. No passengers were involved, nor was there any inconvenience caused.

These incidents were unwelcomed enough but, but for a piece of good fortune on the dark early evening of November 1, 2003, the train could have been involved in a catastrophic accident. Carrying an almost full complement of passengers, once again football supporters on their way home after a match, the train had only a couple of minutes previously passed the point of impact where the dredger **Donald Redford** ploughed into the pier. The track and live rail were, like the pier itself, severely damaged and put out of action for two months. The very thought of up to 48 passengers and a driver suffering the impact is best left unimagined.

Other incidents centre around petty vandalism as on October 24, 2000, when three teenage girls smashed a carriage window, resulting in a £100 repair bill. On a Saturday afternoon in 2007, two youths removed the train from the pierhead station, abandoning it about halfway along the pier. They were subsequently apprehended and arrested in the village. On another occasion in 2007, Mike Omissi, the late-night driver, left the warmth of the office to take the train down the pier, only to find it missing. It was found to be at the seaward end station. How it came to be there remained unexplained; it was assumed a ferry passenger decided not to wait for a driver. These incidents led to the development of a theft prevention device for the tractors.

The train is for carrying passengers and their luggage but on occasions it has embraced other functions including serving as a "mail train" during its early years, carrying the post between the ferry and waiting post office staff at the pier entrance.

Bearing a large placard at the front and decorated with traditional white ribbons, under the guise of the "Honeymoon Express", the train travelled the length of the pier with just two passengers on October 27, 1962, a special service for the newly married Dennis and Diana Hendey. They were on their way to their reception in the restaurant at the end of the pier having just tied the knot at St John's Church in New Road, Hythe. Diana was the daughter of Mr & Mrs E Carter, proprietors of the restaurant.

Several other couples have made their way along the pier in the train on their wedding day, including Gareth Humphries and April Rowed in July 1986, Holly Mitchell, and her bridesmaids on her way to marry James Hayward in Southampton in September 2016, and Phil Bridges and Dierdre Blore in December 2016.

The train has been operated under other guises too. On July 21, 2007, the Hogwarts Express formed a part of Hythe's "Harry Potter Day" in which the various businesses operated Harry Potter themes with witches and wizards visible everywhere to mark the release of the last of J.K. Rowling's Harry Potter series of books, "Harry Potter and the Deathly Hallows".

Children and parents alike rode the "Horror Train" on October 31, 2019, in spooky carriages taken over by witches, ghosts, ghouls, and giant spiders and strewn with cobwebs. A skeleton named Kevin lurked in a corner of one of the carriages and another skeleton actually took the controls of the train from the usual drivers.

It has also taken the role of more serious modes of transport, as both an ambulance and a fire engine. A man who became ill whilst crossing from Southampton was transported up the pier during the mid-1960s and on July 7, 1979, whilst transporting passengers towards the seaward end of the pier the train driver spotted flames between planks of the decking. Having disembarked ferry passengers, the train was quickly turned back towards the fire. The driver, Patrick Ford, and ferry deckhand Ernie Nutbeam acting as firemen lowered buckets over the pier to collect seawater to douse the flames started by a thoughtlessly discarded cigarette.

Skeletal driver (a.k.a. Scott Flood) drives the Horror Train, October 2019 (Alan Titheridge)

The train was at the centre of a controversy between the summers of 1973 and 1974. During July and August 1973, the General Estates Company, owners and operators of the train, restricted access to it to ferry passengers only. Complaints were many and many of those were to the local authorities. The Dibden Parish Council

Kevin escorts 4-year-old Calleigh Parkes on the Horror Train, October 2019 (Alan Titheridge)

took up the issue with the owners. Mr R.R.J. Morgan responded on behalf of the General Estates Company that it was only a temporary measure during the summer months "when people just using the pier tend to overload the trains so that ferry passengers are unable to use them". He added that the train drivers were asked to use their discretion with elderly people.

The issue rumbled on into the spring of 1974 when once again the

The train battles the elements mid 1990s (Margaret Swain, courtesy Sath Naidoo)

council sought clarification on a report of an elderly woman being denied access to the train despite it being relatively empty. Mr Morgan responded, informing the council that his drivers had been told to use common sense during quieter periods.

At this time there was an A-frame board at the entrance of the pier informing the public that the train was for ferry passengers only. Mr Morgan agreed in a letter to the council in July 1974 that the notice could be withdrawn during quieter periods. At a council meeting on July 8, 1974, the Clerk, Mrs Jean Sizer, was instructed to inform the public in her newspaper column in a local free newspaper that elderly people will be conveyed along the pier by train even if they were not ferry passengers. The issue appears to have subsequently faded away.

A one-woman campaign against smoking in the train carriages was rewarded when Mrs Jill Tulip and Mr Morgan found themselves in agreement. A ban was implemented at the start of January 1986. This was advantageous in more than just passenger comfort, it reduced the risk of fire from discarded cigarettes.

There have of course been short interruptions for routine maintenance of both the tractors and rolling stock and for the track and the pier decking beneath, such as in July 2001. Following a routine safety inspection, Hampshire County Council ordered White Horse Ferries to immediately suspend train operations pending emergency repairs to a section of the pier decking below the track. The pier proprietors complied immediately and shunted the train onto the sidings. The work which took ten days to complete also included repairing some lattice beams and the tightening of some of the bolts that had worked loose as the train rumbled over them. The train was back on the track on July 30, 2001.

But for the few aforementioned incidents the Hythe Pier Railway has been running up and down Hythe Pier for almost a century with an unequalled reliability, earning in December 1999 an entry into the Guinness Book of Records (see page 79).

TICKETS, TOLLS & MISCELLANEOUS TRIVIA

TICKETS AND TOLLS

Tickets for the train from the shore end were originally bought from the ferry booking office and collected by the conductor before he indicated to the driver to start the train and commence the journey towards the waiting ferry.

Driver selling tickets at the seaward end station circa 1950s

For shore-bound passengers, tickets were bought from the conductor on boarding the train at the pierhead station and handed over along with any ferry tickets on leaving the pier.

Mr Percy, proprietor of the Hythe Ferry and of the train, was having concerns about the need of the role of conductor as early as 1933, when he pointed out to Mr Roberts, manager of the Hythe Ferry, that the conductor's wages were swallowing up the receipts for using the train.

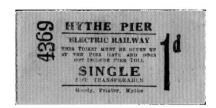

Conductors were employed right up until the outbreak of World War II but at some time shortly thereafter, the conductor's role appears to have been merged with that of the driver.

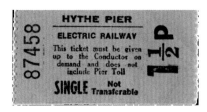

The journey cost one penny, rising to two pence and subsequently three pence in 1970. These days there is no train ticket, the fare is included with that of the ferry or the pier toll.

LIVERY

On arrival at Hythe, the first two carriages were painted grey, with white interiors. A livery of dark green with cream HPR signage was adopted soon afterwards but this was to be changed on numerous occasions over the years.

Subsequently the carriages were painted green below window level and cream above whilst the tractors remained all-over green.

In 1963 both tractors and rolling stock were repainted, like the ferry boats, blue lower and white upper. The process was transitional as there is photographic evidence of both green and blue in the same rake. The HPR signage disappeared at this point.

Blue, 1980s

Red & white, 1998

In 1997 both carriages and tractors were repainted predominantly white but with a narrow lower band of red. In 1998 following a promotional competition the tractors received a "face" whilst one of the driving carriages acquired not one, but two faces. Green was re-adopted in 2000. The cream HPR signage that was re-applied at the same time has subsequently disappeared.

Back to green, 2000

RECORD BREAKER

In December 1999, Hythe's iconic pier railway was given the accolade of entry into the Guinness Book of Records for being "The oldest operating pier train, which has continually served the public, runs on Hythe Pier, Hants, UK and began running in July 1922".

HOW MANY MILES HAS THE TRAIN TRAVELLED?

There is no actual record of the train's movements, so this has to be a best estimated.

CERTIFICATE

The oldest operating pier train, which has continually served the public, runs on Hythe Pier, Hants, UK and began running in July 1922.

Keeper of the Records
GUINESS WORLD RECORDS LTD

The pier is 2100 feet or 700 yards long.

If the train makes 50 trips in a day, the distance travelled would be 35,000 yards or 19.88 miles.

Operating 364 days in a year this would amount to 7,236 miles.

By 2021, the train has been operating on Hythe Pier for 99 years.

Ignoring the relatively few historic days of no service, service trips (staff, maintenance and fuel), the fact that in summer it makes more trips than in winter and not taking into account leap years, 99 years of 7,236 miles amounts to.....

716,364 miles

or 1 ½ round trips to the moon,

or 28 circumferences of the globe,

or the distance covered by 27,552 entrants into a marathon,

or 1,801,144 trips along the pier.

This figure is certainly the minimum. The train has made and still makes very many unscheduled trips. The mileage very probably exceeds...

1,000,000 miles

However it is measured, it is an impressive distance for the small tractors built for operating in a factory site. A real tribute to the contemporary British engineering.

VIDEO STAR

Early in July 2018, the pier and train were featured in the production of a music video for Shannon Gaskin's debut single "Adore", shot by local director Glen Jevon. Some twenty seconds made it to the released version which also features various locations around the New Forest.

Shannon Gaskin, aged 21 at the time, is an English actress / singer, a.k.a Wulfy who plays Camilla Young in the Disney Channel teen drama Penny on M.A.R.S.

Shannon Gaskin
(John Greenwood)

LAWRENCE OF ARABIA

T. E. Lawrence, a.k.a. Lawrence of Arabia, would have travelled along Hythe Pier during his time in Hythe.

He first came to Hythe as a child with his parents and three brothers during the spring of 1894 to a house called Langley Lodge. The family moved on to Oxfordshire three years later. The young Thomas Edward would enjoy days on the beach at Lepe and sail on Southampton Water with his father, a keen sailor and enthusiast for outdoor pursuits.

He didn't return to the area again until the autumn of 1929 when as a serving aircraftsman in the Royal Air Force he assisted his Commanding Officer with arrangements for the Schneider Trophy air race. He lived aboard a private motor yacht, the **Karen**, during the event itself.

After witnessing an R.A.F. flying boat from his station at R.A.F. Mountbatten in Plymouth crash into the sea in February 1931 resulting in the drowning of several crew members despite his best efforts in assisting a rescue, his interest in speeding up seaplane tenders saw him posted to Hythe where Hubert Scott-Paine had set up the British Power Boats Company. He oversaw the construction and trials of a larger and faster seaplane tender for the R.A.F.

Whilst in Hythe he rented rooms at Myrtle Cottage in Shore Road, conveniently located close by the British Power Boats site. He stayed for ten months during 1931 and 1932, returning for another short period later. A blue plaque marking the link between T.E. Lawrence and Myrtle Cottage was unveiled on the property on October 22, 2007.

Myrtle Cottage with blue plaque (Alan Titheridge)

CELEBRITY RIDERS

Unquestionably, King George VI is the most celebrated passenger to have ridden the Hythe Pier Railway. But other "celebrities" have, too, including T.E. Lawrence (Lawrence of Arabia) discussed above.

Sir Oswald Mosely visited the area and used the pier and train. He was a former Member of Parliament representing both the Conservative and Labour parties and serving as an independent before establishing and becoming leader of the British Union of Fascists.

Sir Bernard and Lady Docker were frequent visitors to the New Forest and often used the train to get to their luxury yacht, the **Shemara**, moored off the pier. Sir Bernard Docker was a successful, but controversial businessman, his wife Norah, a celebrated socialite. Hardly a day passed without them being featured in the glossy magazines of the 1950s and 1960s or splashed across the gossip columns of the national newspapers of the time. They were the reality superstars of their day.

Dan Snow on Hythe Pier, December 2016

Historian and television presenter Dan Snow was on the pier in December 2016 to lend a hand in publicising the plight of the Hythe Ferry service and the need to save it as it was threatened with closure. He took the train to the end of the pier and back as a part of the publicity, later "tweeting" a photograph of the train and adding "The world's oldest pier train. Still carrying passengers. Worth saving".

English actress and singer Shannon Gaskin recorded a music video on the train in 2018 as detailed earlier in this chapter.

Actress Su Pollard, best known for her role as Peggy Ollerenshaw, the scatty chalet maid in the television series Hi-di-Hi and who also starred in the television series You Rang M'Lord? and Oh, Doctor Beeching between 1980 and 1997 was a visitor during the early years of this century as was Jeffrey Holland, who played Spike Dixon in Hi-di-Hi as well as appearing in It Ain't Half Hot Mum and co-starring with Su Pollard in You Rang M'Lord? and Oh, Dr. Beeching who came across by ferry with his wife, actress Judy Buxton, both riding the train up the pier to visit the Hythe Marina.

Larger than life actor Brian Blessed has also ridden the train during a visit to the area.

There are probably others too. Sir Christopher Cockerill, inventor of the hovercraft lived in Hythe as did Tommy Cooper, television magician and comedian who was an apprentice shipwright at the British Power Boats Company prior to the Second World War. It is hard to imagine neither rode the pier train.

SIBLINGS
An indeterminate number, but at least 14, battery-electric locomotives were ordered by the Ministry of Munitions in 1917 from the Brush Electrical Engineering Co. Ltd of Loughborough for deployment at its munition factories at Avonmouth, Gretna and Queensferry.

The tractors still running on the Hythe Pier are known to be two of a batch of six built under order number 21222.

Sadly, Brush records are long since destroyed, otherwise known detail: Nos. 16237, 16238, 16239 and 16240 – each to Ministry of Munitions,

Gretna / Dornoch.

16302 – HMEF (His Majesty's Explosives Factory) Avonmouth. Sold to General Estates Co Ltd for use on Hythe Pier in 1920. Commenced operating July 1922, still operating 2021.

16303 – Although not certain, believed to be HMEF Queensferry (Flintshire). Nothing further is known of its early history until February 3, 1950 when records show the sale of two battery-electric locomotives (16303 and 16306) by E Smith & Sons, Chester to Thos. W. Ward, Sheffield who immediately sold them on to W.O. Williams, Harlech. They were moved on to Manod Quarry, Blaenau Ffestiniog where 16303 was used to haul large slabs of slate up steep inclines until 1979. Acquired by Rich Morris in 1981 and subsequently by Peter Smith in February 1998, when it was moved to the Amberley Museum in West Sussex. After much restoration it was successfully made mobile and is now presented as MoM3.

16304 - HMEF Avonmouth. Sold to General Estates Co Ltd for use on Hythe Pier. Known to be operational in November 1932 but subsequently cannibalised for spares. It is known to have been

16303 (Martin Haywood)

16305 at the National Slate Museum (Terry Wallace)

16307 at Hythe Pier (Alan Titheridge)

16304 Identification plate attached to cannibalised motor discovered May 2021
(John Greenwood)

permanently out of commission in August 1935. After more than 8 decades, the shell of a long forgotten motor was discovered in the Hythe Ferry workshop complete with original 16304 identification plate in May 2021.

16305 – Believed to be that exhibited at the National Slate Museum (formerly Welsh Slate Museum) at Llanberis in North Wales (in 2020). Having possibly been deployed at HMEF Avonmouth, offered for sale in 1920, acquired by B.E. White Ltd who had it overhauled and modified. Sold on to Votty & Bowydd slate quarry at Blaenau Ffestiniog, where it was further modified and joined by another (unspecified) unit from George Cohen & Sons (nothing further appears to be known about this unit). Upon the closure of the Votty & Bowydd quarry in 1962, it was bought by Aberllefenni Slate Quarries Ltd and employed at their Foel Grochan quarry. Early in 1977 the tractor batteries died, so it was abandoned on-site. By 1982 it had made its way to a cutting shed at Aberllefenni before being bought by the museum in 1983. During the 1980s it was sent to Cammell Laird shipbuilders at Birkenhead for (partial) restoration. At some point after Cammell Laird went into receivership in 2001, the tractor unit was returned to the museum and stored at Gilfach Ddu. It was put on display in 2006. Subsequently restored to working condition.

16306 – See 16303. Known to have been no more than a shell in 1954. A part of its bodywork frame was used in the restoration of 16303.

16307 - HMEF Avonmouth. Sold to General Estates Co Ltd for use on Hythe Pier. Commenced operating July 1922, still operating 2021.

16329, 16330 and 16331 – No known details of deployment.

16307 at Hythe Pier (Alan Titheridge)

TRAIN DRIVER KNOWLEDGE TEST - ANSWERS

1 – C   (Disengage the brake wheel)

2 – C   (Check your mirror)

3 – C   (A luminous bridge formed in a gap between two electrodes)

4 – C   (Gradually using brake point markers)

5 – A   (The solenoid is deactivated and power to the motor is cut)

6 – C   (Tractor unit)

7 – B   (Are the train lights on)

8 – C   (Move the selector handle to the first position to disengage the brake wheel)

9 – C   (Tractor unit)

10 – 10

11 – 10mm

12 – 100 amp

13 – B   (Report fault by paperwork system and contact an engineer and seek advice)

14 – C   (Ensure the trackside power is switched off)

15 – C   (For both of the above)

16 – A   (0-45 and drops down to 10 amps)

17 – D   (other – there are 28 numbered to 29, there being no number 13).

OTHER ROLLING STOCK

In March 1922, Mr T B Percy suggested to both his engineer, Mr Gerald Yorke, and his Hythe Manager, Mr J Roberts, that the two four-wheeled luggage trucks, each with two flatbed decks that were being used on the tracks laid in 1909, could be adapted for use on the Hythe Pier Railway. These were 7 feet 6 inches long x 3 feet 6 inches wide and had been used to carry all manner of items, and people, along the track on the northern side of the decking. Mr Percy further suggested that these trucks could each be coupled between one of the tractors and the carriages.

Circa 1922-23, early photograph showing luggage truck, with two tractors and first two carriages

Only one of these trucks is still in existence and is used daily. A clue as to the demise of the other can be found in a letter from Mr Percy to Mr Yorke on August 24, 1922. Mr Percy wrote: "You have heard of the train pushing the luggage truck over the end of the pier, I expect."

Luggage truck (Photograph courtesy Hythe Pier Heritage Association)

The staff were still learning just two months after the start of the train's inauguration, experiencing among other difficulties that of communication. The train was operating with a tractor at each end

Luggage truck (Photograph courtesy Hythe Pier Heritage Association)

at this time, the driving carriages not yet having been ordered. A man was positioned in the front tractor to apply the brake in the event of an obstruction, if necessary; the driver was in the rear tractor. Mr Roberts was in the front tractor and applied the brake when the train met an idle luggage truck at the first landing. There was no pre-arranged signal for such an incident, so the driver was unaware of Mr Roberts' intention to brake, the outcome being an overload blowing a fuse. A porter replaced the fuse but with Mr Roberts having had released the brake, the train immediately lurched forward, pushing the truck off the pier. No record has been traced of its recovery.

Luggage truck (Photograph courtesy Hythe Pier Heritage Association)

A steel tank truck (bowser) with a wooden frame was acquired, possibly sometime during the 1930s, to transport fuel oil for the ferry boats at the pierhead. A replacement for the original tank truck was introduced during the 1970s, which in turn was replaced by an all-steel unit measuring 7 feet

Steel tank truck (Alan Titheridge)

6 inches x 3 feet 6 inches wide with a capacity of 1500 litres of fuel oil towards the end of the first decade of the 21st Century.

DRIVERS

The "Locomotive" magazine for February 15, 1919, wrote of the tractor units that they do not "require skilled labour to look after and drive them".

The feature continued: "Any man of ordinary intelligence can properly care for a (battery) locomotive after a few hours tuition. There is no excuse for the locomotive to stand idle should the regular driver be away, for it is a simple matter to have one or two men, usually on other work, trained to drive it."

Unknown driver, circa 1920s

This might have been the case in the controlled environment of a shore factory but the prevailing conditions on Hythe Pier, a totally different and sometimes unpredictable environment, would suggest otherwise. With up to 48 passengers at any one time and variations in the weather, driving the Hythe Pier train has required a greater responsibility.

Just how many have driven the train along the pier is impossible to ascertain. This chapter looks at just a few of the men and the one woman who have.

On July 1, 1939, there were four drivers on the wages sheet: A Parsons, W Longman, C Waterman and C Randall. For the week ending July 1, 1939, they were paid £3 19s 1d, £3 13s 9d, £4 2s 3d and £3 7s 1d gross, respectively.

T Longman and Len Pearce, who went on to be the driver who drove the train with King George VI as a passenger in 1944, were listed as conductors, earning £2 19s 0d and £3 9s 6d gross, respectively.

Len Cavill
(Courtesy Pauline Smith)

LEN CAVILL

Len Cavill joined the General Estates Company during the early summer of 1954. His primary job was as engineer on one or other of the Hotspur ferry boats. However, he was a regular driver of the train, too.

At about 11pm on July 14, 1955, having delivered passengers from the ferry to the shore-end pier station, he was in the office when he noticed an altercation close by the pier entrance. He saw a police constable surrounded by five men who had just left the pier, one of whom had punched the constable, knocking him to the ground. Len, who had served in the Police War Reserve at Hythe during the hostilities, immediately went to the aid of the constable and assisted him in making an arrest.

The magistrate at the court hearing of the assailant who had delivered the punch, in expressing his appreciation for Len Cavill's brave action, said: "He should be congratulated for his gallant assistance."

An inspector at Hythe also praised Len's action. He said: "Had it not been for the assistance given to PC Clarke by Mr Cavill, there is no doubt this attack would have developed into a much more serious offence."

Len was also a retained fireman at Hythe Fire Station.

Len was born in 1905 and passed away, aged 63, in 1968. He married his wife Ada in 1928 and together they had three children, June, Alan and Eileen. He was still an employee of the General Estates Company at the time of his death; his death certificate listing his occupation as "Engineer (Estuarial Ferry)".

Len Cavill
(Courtesy Pauline Smith)

ROY DAVIS

Robert "Roy" Davis is arguably the most remembered of all the post-war drivers. He was extremely popular, not just with all his passengers but throughout the village. He was a regular patron at the Lord Nelson pub in the High Street; his portrait hung in one of the bars for very many years following his retirement.

A young Roy Davis, circa early 1930s (Courtesy Terry Phillips)

Roy was christened Robert Wright Davis. In an interview with the Southern Evening Echo from his home in Hobart Drive, Hythe, marking his retirement, Roy explained: "I was given the name at school and it has stuck ever since." Roy retired through poor health after 27 years' service, the great majority of it driving the train, on January 5, 1973.

He joined the General Estates Company in 1945 after having recovered from a serious wound received whilst with the Royal Artillery fighting in France. Before the war, he worked as a gardener at three of Hythe's great houses, firstly Mount House, then West Cliff Hall and finally Langdown House.

To mark his retirement, Mr Fred Abrahams, the yard bosun, presented Roy with a pipe and an alarm clock on behalf of his work colleagues.

Roy Davis and a budding young successor, 1950s (Courtesy Jackie Major)

In an "Echo News Feature" published on August 17, 1977, Roy gave an in-depth look at what it was what like to drive the train. When asked what it was like to drive, he responded: "Quite easy." The only difficult part was stopping as "the wind would push you along and you had to be careful".

Roy recalled when his wages were 1s 6d per hour and he would sometimes be on duty until nearly midnight. Tips were always welcome, especially those from Sir Bernard and Lady Docker. The contemporary socialites would hire the train for one shilling to take them to the end of the pier to their motor yacht **Shemara**, moored just off the structure. "One good thing about the Dockers," he said, "they were always good tippers."

Roy went on to remember Sir Oswald Mosley, a former MP and leader of the British Fascist Movement, saying of him: "He was always a perfect gentleman."

Roy concluded in saying: "People always used to say they thought I had a boring job. I never thought so. There were always so many interesting people."

Roy Davis issuing a ticket, circa late 1960s (Courtesy Jackie Major)

Roy Davis checking all clear, 1960s (Courtesy Terry Phillips)

Roy was born in Hythe on June 28, 1911, the eldest of five children. He never married and lived with his mother in St John's Street, Hythe, before moving with her to Hobart Drive, where he continued to live after she died. Roy passed away at Ashurst Hospital on October 2, 1982, aged 71.

LEN PEARCE

Len Pearce was working as a conductor on the Hythe Pier Railway when war broke out in 1939. Having been born in 1893, he was too old for active service so continued to work on Hythe Pier during the hostilities, advancing to become a driver.

He retired from the General Estates Company after 38 years of service on September 30, 1965, aged 72.

The "highlight of (his) career" came just before D-Day in 1944 when he drove the train carrying His Majesty King George VI along the pier. During a brief conversation with Len, according to Roy Davis in the 1977 Echo "Newsfeature", the King told him that he "had travelled all over the world but had never seen such a funny old train".

ERNIE 'TAFF' CLARK

Hailing from South Wales and having arrived in Hythe with his wife and their children in 1963, Ernest John Clark started working for the General Estates Company in 1965. He had previously worked in a colliery in the Rhondda Valley but was advised his occupation was contributing to his ill-health. His doctor recommended he should be breathing clean sea air and he was fortunate to find a job with it in abundance. He loved his job and the camaraderie at the Hythe Ferry, particularly when driving the train. He was immensely proud when promoted to the role of Pier Master.

Ernie Clarke
(Courtesy Paul Wathan and Donna Goodwin)

Known to his colleagues as "Taff", Ernie (born May 1, 1908) passed away aged 90 in June 1998. Along with that of his wife Mary, his name is perpetuated, engraved on a plank on Hythe Pier.

ALAN POWELL

Alan Powell became a train driver shortly after the retirement of Roy Davis, a hard act to follow.

In the August 17, 1977 "Echo Newsfeature", Alan agreed with Roy Davis that the job wasn't boring "because there was always something happening". Alan added: "As long as a driver

Alan Powell
(Courtesy Laura Logan)

realises this isn't Inter-City, treats the old train with respect and remembers to keep the speed down and watch the wind, he'll be OK."

Alan, who also worked as a ferry crewman, was born on September 17, 1940, the third child of Bill and Elsie Powell. He had two older brothers and a younger sister. Alan passed away, aged 65, on May 29, 2006.

PATRICK FORD

Patrick Ford, then 51 years of age, was driving the train in September 1979 when he was interviewed by Anne Edwards for her regular "Waterside Diary" feature in the Southern Evening Echo. The interest was not so much for his day job, but for his artistic prowess.

Patrick was quoted as saying: "I have enjoyed painting since I was a child. At school, the teachers would not let me go in for painting competitions because they said I would win too easily."

Patrick Ford
(Courtesy Martin Ford)

He continued: "I never wanted to take up painting full-time and never had any formal art training. I like to sit down and paint when I feel inspired."

For a very many years one of Patrick's paintings hung in Hythe Hospital. He was also passionate about flowers and was "very proud of his home-grown orchids".

Patrick passed away at the age of 87 in 2014.

JACK KING

Jack King joined the General Estates Company in 1985. His first role was running the old ticket office at the Town Quay alongside his brother Percy. Following the demolition of the ticket office and waiting room as part of the Town Quay redevelopment during the late 1980s and the subsequent closure of the temporary manned ticketing facility at the Town Quay during the early 1990s, he briefly worked as a crewman on the **Hotspur IV** before taking on the role of train driver.

Jack King
(Courtesy Peter King)

Jack was born in Southampton, the youngest of seven children, on December 1, 1930. He served an apprenticeship with Vosper as a shipwright and was called up for National Service before getting married to Betty on April 2, 1955. During the late 1950s he began working for Monsanto at its Hardley plant, remaining there until its closure before going on to several jobs including driving the Hythe Hopper bus service.

Jack passed away on March 10, 2012.

Jack's son is Peter King, the founding chairman of the Hythe Pier Heritage Association and the early driving force behind the organisation's plans to restore Hythe Pier and its iconic railway to former glories. Peter reminisces of his father: "He gave me my first experience on the pier in 1965 as a four-year-old, and it remains one of my earliest childhood memories, fishing at a point beyond the first shelter. I can remember it as if it were yesterday, just one of the many reasons it means so much to me."

GERRY BARTON

Gerry Barton, a former welder, was born in 1949. He started on the ferry boats in 1990 and transferred to driving the train in 1994.

Gerry Barton

He told a newspaper reporter on the awarding of the Guinness record in 1999 that driving the train was "a great job", before adding: "You get to see so many different things throughout the year."

In a further newspaper interview, this time the Daily Telegraph on November 11, 2006, he said of the carriages: "They were built for much smaller people than we are now. Sometimes when passengers are jumping in, they do not take into account how narrow the doors are. Every now and again I look in my rear-view mirror and see arms and legs sticking out."

Gerry left White Horse Ferries in 2012.

SARAH MARSDEN

Sarah Marsden has the distinction of being the only female train driver in the history of the Hythe Pier Railway.

Sarah Marsden (Sath Naidoo)

Sarah had been a regular commuter when she spotted a handwritten notice in the ticket-office window advertising for an office administrator. She knocked the door, had a chat over a coffee and the rest, as it is said, is history.

Sarah explains what happened next: "After some time in the position of office administrator/ticket sales clerk, I was gradually inveigled to help with the staff rota to keep the boats and train running on a day-to-day basis. As many of the staff (excluding a core full-time boat crew and train crew) were retired part-timers, it became more and more complicated to keep a 3-week rolling rota going. In the end I offered to learn to act as 3rd Hand – essentially available to work during rush hour or exceptional passenger numbers. It was easy to keep a uniform in the office, and if a 3rd hand on the rota failed to turn up for shift due to unforeseen circumstances I could change into uniform, trot down to the boat and take over until someone else was available. Obviously, I had to train to be a fully endorsed crew member, able to undertake any duties and fully conversant with all safe practices in starting, running, and shutting down the two vessels, **Great Expectations** and **Hotspur IV**."

One day Sarah returned from a summer holiday to be informed that a train driver had been taken ill, and much to the reservations of the full-time train driving crew she was given an immediate "crash course" education in train driving.

Sarah remembers: "At the time, of course, I received a lot of ribbing from the core train drivers! Pink L Plates appeared! "Brake Now" notices were painted on the track, but at heart, they were all (I think) rather proud to play a part in teaching me the secrets of pier train driving!"

Sarah also recalls: "The train is, indeed, subject to the weather! Frost, wind, rain, and snow all play a vital part in how the train should be managed. The pier was gritted in frosty conditions by running the train gently down the pier whilst flinging shovels of grit out of the door. On one occasion, a snowstorm swept in whilst one of our regular 90-year-old Hythe residents was taking his daily constitutional. Gerry (Barton), the train driver on that day, responded to my request and took the train down the pier and rescued Frank."

It was not only Sarah's colleagues who commented on her train driving skills but some of her passengers did so, too.

Again, Sarah explains: "Some passengers are nervous about traversing the pier and anxious to confirm that you know when to stop. My answer was usually that if you felt a slight bump, I may have brushed up against the buffers, but if your feet started getting wet . . ."

Sarah was forced to leave White Horse Ferries (at the time, the ferry, pier and train owner) due to family circumstances shortly after the Donald Redford incident.

However, she says: "It was a wonderful time in my life. I give local history talks now, and when I talk about the ferry and train, I am most proud of the fact that I was the first lady train driver on the oldest continually operating pier train in the world!"

MIKE OMISSI

Mike Omissi, a former steel stockholding company owner, moved to Hythe in 2004. He drove the train from 2006 until 2015 but returned to the job in 2016. He finally retired in June 2018.

JOHN PIPE

After 20 years in the Royal Navy, leaving in 1992, John Pipe did a variety of jobs before joining White Horse Ferries in 2010. He started on the boats but gained further experience manning the Town Quay. He was often asked if he would like to drive the pier train but repeatedly declined.

*Mike Omissi
(Nell Whiting)*

John Pipe (Alan Titheridge)

In 2016, John was again offered the role of driving the train; this time he accepted. He told the author of this book: "It is an experience for me that I had thought would not appeal to me. I have come to love the experience of driving this excellent piece of history up and down the pier."

John, who was born in Romford, Essex, in February 1953 and moved to Hythe in 1977, maintains the mooring ropes and makes up new ones for the boats between trips down the pier.

John's self-acknowledged lack of height causes amusement among his colleagues. He explains: "I am the only driver who has to put the brake on at the seaward end of the train when arriving back at the main station, this stops it from rolling a yard or so to the low point at the end of the track, coupled with a short length of old pier planking being placed at the mounting point for that end of the train, giving me the opportunity to get up to the driver's cab without having to overreach for the grab handle to assist in getting up into the driver's cab."

SCOTT FLOOD

Scott Flood came by the role of train driver by accident. Having retired after 39 years of shift work with Esso Petroleum in 2016 at the age of 60, he found himself with his wife Caz at an HPHA fundraising event where he was told that the pier train was not running because there was no driver available. Caz flippantly remarked that Scott would volunteer to drive if ever needed. A day or two later he was at the pier and told to learn how to drive the train as soon as possible. He did just that, took the test and at the age of 61 in 2017, he embarked upon a new career.

Scott Flood
(Courtesy Scott Flood)

Scott says: "Working down the pier is really great fun, a real family atmosphere, everyone so friendly. I have gotten to know lots of regular travellers. During the summer there is a lot of people from all over the world visiting and I enjoy talking to them about the local area and the pier and train. I don't consider it a job, more of a hobby."

The highlight of his time on the pier to date was in October 2019 when he was the man behind the skeletal mask driving the Halloween "Horror Train".

Scott's parents, Geoff and Dot Flood, ran the café at the end of the pier between 1986 and 1989.

ROLL CALL

As written in the first paragraph of this chapter just how many have driven the train along the pier is impossible to ascertain. Listed below are a few, including relief drivers, of those known to have driven the train with passengers aboard.

Barton, Gerry	Longman, Tommy
Bullen, Geoff	Longman, William
Cavill, Len	Maidment, Fred
Chambers, Mike	Marsden, Sarah
Clark, Earnest "Taff"	Marston, Jack
Clinton, Ian	Moody, Dave
Clinton, Richard	Munday, Mark
Crosby, Ken	Naidoo, Sath
Davis, Peter	Omissi, Mike
Davis, Robert "Roy"	Orchard, Colin
Derham, Maurice "Jack"	Parsons, Arthur
Dunstan, Tony	Pearce, Len
Flood, Scott	Phillips, Thomas
Ford, Patrick	Pipe, John
Holmquest, Paul	Powell, Alan
Hosey, C	Randall, Charles
Jennings, Vic	Randall, William
King, Dave	Rayment, Lee
King, Jack	Titheridge, Colin
Langley, Peter	Town, Fred
Locker, Ian	Waterman, C
London, Paul	West, Len

MEMORIES & ANECDOTES

Everyday life, whether on the Hythe Pier, Train and Ferry or anywhere else, often passes us by but occasionally there is that something that sets one day apart. Something, often something trivial, will stick in the memory, often longer and sometimes more affectionately, than something more important, to be recalled sometime later maybe raising a smile and a warm glow from our pasts. The mind can choose how we remember; to embellish, to simplify or tell it the way it was.

The Hythe Pier train is held in great affection, not just throughout the local community but among those formerly of it now living further afield; here are just a few moments as recalled by a few of those who share that fondness.

JOY MUNDAY OF HYTHE, HAMPSHIRE ...
GROWN UP LEGS

"I used to love riding the train as a child. It always fascinated me how grown ups' legs used to move from side to side in time to the clackety-clack of the train. I couldn't wait to grow up so mine would do the same."

SANDRA BARNES OF FRESHWATER, IOW...
ENORMOUS KNICKERS

"Back in 1993, on my way to work and heavily pregnant with my first child, I was on the train to enable me to catch the ferry. The train was approximately three quarters of the way down Hythe Pier when it stopped and everybody on board was asked to alight as the train had developed an electrical fire. As the train had stopped prior to its normal destination, all passengers had to climb through the wire fencing that separated the track from the pier. As I was pregnant, other passengers pulled apart the wire to assist me in climbing through. It was very kind of them but afterwards, to my horror, I discovered my maternity dress which was akin to a marquee had revealed my ever so enormous pregnancy knickers. This memory will always stay with me and probably everyone else that was on the train at the time."

GEOFF BULLEN OF DIBDEN PURLIEU, HAMPSHIRE ... ONLY 15

"I started my fitter and turner apprenticeship in 1967. I worked in the shed at the end of the yard by the slipway. During my time working for General Estates, I was taught how to drive the train. I was only 14 when I started, probably only 15 when I drove the train."

BOO HOLMQUEST OF FAWLEY, HAMPSHIRE ... OFF THE RAILS

"My husband Paul worked on the Hythe Ferry from 1995-1998 and drove the train on and off during that time. One Cowes Week he and the rest of the crew had permission to drive the ferry with the families and a small group of close friends to watch the display of fireworks. I believe John Malkinson was the skipper that night. The weather started off well then it poured down with rain. John navigated his way back in the pitch black, being careful to avoid the odd mad person sat in a rowing boat with no lights. When we arrived back at Hythe Pier we all loaded onto the train. I think the driver that night was Gerry (Barton) and it started to trundle down the track, however we got so far along the track, remembering the pouring rain when the train came off the rails. The train had to be lifted back on to the tracks ready for service the next morning, so all of us men and women rolled up our sleeves and put our backs into manhandling the train and carriages back on to the rails for the next day. We were (me included) absolutely drenched through but it was business as usual the next day."

LIZ DAINES (FORMERLY BARTLETT) OF FELIXSTOWE, SUFFOLK ... HEALTH AND SAFETY!

"My dad used to drink in the Nelson with Roy (Davis) who used to drive the train in the late 60s and early 70s. Very occasionally he used to let me and my sister sit up in the cab with him and "drive" the train down the pier. So exciting for a 6 and 7 years old. Health and safety didn't exist at all then."

RICHARD KIRK OF TEWANTIN, QUEENSLAND, AUSTRALIA... MIND MY BEER

"In the 60s a little old guy called Roy (Davis) used to drive the train. He used to come into my Dad's pub, the Lord Nelson, and sit in the little bar with a beer every time the train was at the land end. He used to leave his glass on the end of the bar for when he returned."

LORRAINE MCAUSLAND OF HYTHE, HAMPSHIRE ... GIRL MEETS BOY

"My husband (Duncan) and I first saw each other in one of the carriages, he was 16, I was 18, in 1989. We both worked for Lloyds Bank and were on a course together. He was travelling with his mum who worked in Debenhams. We didn't see each other again for many years until we worked together in 1993 when we became boyfriend and girlfriend. We married in 1996 and are still married now after 24 years with two daughters. They both know the story of our first meeting and groan whenever it is mentioned."

GRAHAM RICHMOND OF HOLBURY, HAMPSHIRE ... NOW YOU ARE A REAL COWBOY

"The pier repair gang were returning back down the pier on the train. John, the apprentice welder, was riding stood on the parcel trolley at the back of the train facing Big Kevin who was riding on a small platform between the last carriage and the middle carriage. As usual the normal good-humoured banter between them commenced until John said something which upset Big Kevin. In a rage, Big Kevin crawled on all fours across the roof of the last carriage to confront John and give him a friendly warning. The sight of a giant man crawling across the roof of a train as it trundled down Hythe Pier was reminding everyone of the old John Wayne films and giving rights to the gang to shout, 'Now you are a real cowboy, Kevin'."

IRENE FERGUSON OF DUNFERMLINE, FIFE ... EVERY PENNY COUNTED

"Back in the 1960s my Dad, Mum, brother, sister, and myself travelled on the train every Saturday, for years, to catch the ferry to Southampton for the weekly shop. My Dad used to walk the pier to save the fare. Every penny counted back then."

JENNY GRAY RANDALL OF KURANDA, QUEENSLAND, AUSTRALIA ... THEN CAME THE DILEMMA

"I used to work in Southampton so used to travel every day on the ferry. I remember the times, in the thick of winter, getting off the ferry in sleet and perishing arctic wind. I'd get to the train to find it already full. Then came the dilemma ... wait for the train to come back and be frozen to the bone by the time it did or start walking. On other occasions in thick fog when I couldn't see the Hythe end of the pier, I'd hear the train trundling along ages before it appeared out of the gloom."

EMILY BLACK OF HYTHE, HAMPSHIRE ... A WHOLE CARRIAGE FOR US

"I got married at the registry office in Southampton. We lived in Hythe, so I got ready with my bridal party at my house. Then most of my immediate family came to meet us at my house and we walked to the pier together. They had reserved a whole carriage for us on the train so we all got to ride together. It was really incredible, and I couldn't have been more grateful for all the help they gave to me when booking. It was a last minute decision, because we didn't realise we'd booked our wedding the weekend of the boat show and we all know what the traffic can be like getting into town. It saved my whole wedding morning and we all had so much fun riding the train and the ferry."

KEITH WITCHELL OF DIBDEN PURLIEU, HAMPSHIRE ... NARROWLY SAVED BY HIS KNEES

"I used the pier during my school years between 1970 and 1975. There were a number of schools in Southampton using the (ferry) service. During these many happy years it was generally accepted that it was the adult paying passengers that got to ride the train, while us kids walked the pier or ran it if our bus had come in late. On one occasion during the winter months when there was a thick frost on the boards (which made walking very difficult) one of our party almost ended up in the drink after slipping onto his back and sliding under the railings; he was narrowly saved by his knees striking the bottom handrail. On the way home in the evening the same rules applied, and it was our chance again to prove how fast we could run with our heavily laden school bags to catch a ride on the awaiting bus before it left."

GEOFF BECK OF POOLE, DORSET ...
DON'T DANGLE YOUR FEET

"When I was a very small boy, some 50 years back, I spent summer breaks at Hythe with my grandparents. When we rode the train, I held my Granddad's hand very tight as I was worried about falling into the sea through the board gaps, which seemed huge with so small feet, and being much closer to the ground than I am now. I was too small to see over the window ledge so only saw water, so always looked to the walkway side to make sure the train hadn't sunk. And, in those days, if you asked really nicely, the driver let you sit on the flat luggage carriage, as long as you stayed cross-legged and didn't dangle your feet over the edge. Health & Safety would do their nut if you did that today."

DAVID BARLOW OF CHESTER, CHESHIRE ...
THE TRAIN NEVER STOOD A CHANCE

"As a boy I used to wait until the train was fully loaded and then set off at breakneck speed being spurred on by the 'clack clack noise of the train in hot pursuit and getting louder behind me. In my mind it was some terrible beast chasing me.

"When I left school, I joined Southampton Technical College and the ferry, pier and train became a regular feature of my life, travelling from Holbury. Quite often (off the ferry) as I walked towards the train, I could see the No.39 bus already waiting at the other end of the pier and threatening to leave at any moment. Under these circumstances the train was quickly ignored as I would run down the pier as fast as I could. The train never stood a chance, and I would leave it in my wake, sometimes, but often the bus would leave before I was even half-way down. I then faced the ignominy of the train trundling passed, full of fellow students, as I gave up the chase and walked breathless the rest of the way.

"My Uncle Alan (Powell) drove the train for many years, and he would always break into a grin and wave as I walked down the pier and he passed me in the opposite direction."

THE HEARTBEAT OF HYTHE

HYTHE PIER TRAIN
ON POSTCARDS

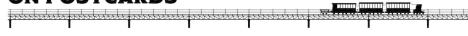

With just about everybody having a mobile phone camera about their person, giving them the opportunity to share an image instantly these days, the picture postcard has become something of a thing of the past. The images of bygone days captured on postcards are of a moment in time that will last far beyond the lifespan of most modern digital images. This chapter of this book records some of the picture postcards depicting the Hythe Pier Railway of the post-World War II era.

HYTHE, HAMPSHIRE

Herald Publishing postcard Hythe, Hampshire circa 2012
(Alan Titheridge collection)

*Anonymous postcard The Pier Express 1379 circa mid 1950s
(Alan Titheridge collection)*

*Anonymous postcard Electric Train, Hythe Pier P21 circa late 1950s
(Alan Titheridge collection)*

*Harvey Barton postcard E11A Electric Train on Hythe Pier, Hampshire circa mid 1960s
(Alan Titheridge collection)*

E11E *Pier and Electric Train*

*Harvey Barton postcard E11E Pier and Electric Train circa mid 1960s
(Alan Titheridge collection)*

*Dearden & Wade postcard 1199 Electric Train, Hythe Pier circa early 1960s
(Alan Titheridge collection)*

*Dearden & Wade multi-view postcard Greetings from Hythe 4731, used, postmarked
August 7, 1967 (Alan Titheridge collection)*

*Direct View postcard The Pier Train, Hythe BT4115, circa 1971
(Alan Titheridge collection)*

*J. Arthur Dixon postcard Hythe Ferry Train L6-SP.7139 circa 1976
(Alan Titheridge collection)*

G.G. Pictures postcard Hythe Ferry Train 1994 (Alan Titheridge collection)

*J. Salmon multi-view postcard Hythe - New Forest circa late 1990s
(Alan Titheridge collection)*

INTO THE 21ST CENTURY, UNCERTAIN TIMES

The awarding of an entry into the Guinness Book of Records in December 1999 could have been a short-lived accolade.

Mr Lloyd Lay, a director of White Horse Ferries, on confirmation of the entry said, "Getting into the record books is certainly going to put us and Hythe on the map", but just four years later, in 2003, consideration was being given to replacing it with a modern "people mover".

PPM Class 139 railcar with heritage outline (Courtesy Parry People Movers)

The staff magazine "Parry News" issue 37, October 2004, of Midlands-based company Parry People Movers, revealed the company had been completing a study commissioned by South Hampshire Rapid Transport Network and funded by Hampshire County Council in conjunction with White Horse Ferries when the dredger **Donald Redford** catastrophically collided with the pier. The proposal was to replace the aging pier train with a broader gauge Parry People Mover, to continue on embedded track right into the heart of the village to meet up with an extended park and ride facility with a view to removing people from their cars and consequently increasing ferry passenger numbers.

Parry People Movers have provided such facilities throughout the United Kingdom. Mr John Parry, chairman of Parry People Movers, explained to the author of this book in October 2018 that the proposal was to supply a tramway shuttle using metal Waybeam technology of at least two PPM Class 139 railcars with heritage outlines to blend in with the historic aspect of the pier and village centre. The Class 139 railcar is available in a number of derivations suitable for purpose. Fuelled by either compressed natural or liquefied petroleum gas, the vehicles are capable of speeds up to 35 mph, but restrictors would have been applied, taking into account the location.

Depending on point of view, the **Donald Redford** disaster arguably prevented another. The lightweight tram system was not to be.

During its 22 years tenure of the Hythe Ferry and with it the pier and train, White Horse Ferries had to endure many obstacles and incidents impacting upon the operation of the business. From a 740% hike in business rates imposed in 2004 (reduced to just under 400% on appeal and a petition of 15,000 signatures supporting the ferry company) to the calamity of the dredger **Donald Redford** incident, drains on its cash flow kept on coming and at a time when passenger numbers were falling.

Your Name Here (Donna Wilson)

To combat this the ferry boats **Hythe Hotspur** and **New Forester** were sold, leaving the ferry service to be operated by the **Great Expectations** with the aging **Hotspur IV** as back up. Maintenance of the pier decking was subsidised by the popular sponsor-a-plank scheme in which the public were invited to "buy a plank" with an engraved inscription, perpetuating their name for its longevity.

Operating a pier railway is an expensive business. White Horse Ferries, however, maintained the tractors and carriages to the required standards of mechanical reliability using quality components to ensure service efficiency and passenger safety.

This maintenance, both routine and essential, between 1997 and 2015, included:

      8 Train wheels @ £134 each
      8 Train wheel tyres @ £92.50 each
      2 Traction Motor rebuilds @ £4,355 each
      Train tapered/roller bearings –
      16 x 1 ¾" SKF @ average price £82
      16 x 1 ¾" Hoffman @ average price £125
      3 sets Niphan electrical connection plugs @ £409 each
      24 Tractor unit Triplex drive chains @ £230 each length
      4 GRP Roof for carriages @ £400 each
      2 Drive coach Royal Jackson re-wire @ £1,300
      2 Tractor unit Royal Jackson re-wire @ £800
      One reel 7 core power cable @ £500

Many of the components are unique, having to be hand-made in a mixture of imperial and metric dimensions, thus inflating cost. In addition to these costs there was that for glass, timber, fixings, and consumables as well as for track maintenance.

By 2014, the ferry service was a one-boat operation, the ailing **Hotspur IV** having been retired. The **Great Expectations** was herself becoming increasingly unreliable, with regular breakdowns necessitating by-the-hour charters of replacement boats. The ill-fated introduction of the unpopular trimaran vessel **Uriah Heep** compounded issues when in 2016 she ploughed into the pier causing extensive damage. The travelling public was understandably voting with its feet, passenger numbers were dropping alarmingly.

By the time White Horse Ferries issued redundancy notices to its staff in

Carriage maintenance (Margaret Swain courtesy Sath Naidoo)

October 2016, when it stated publicly that it was making "unsustainable" losses and that it was "unlikely" to continue operating the ferry service, both the pier and the train, although working efficiently and safely, were looking much the worse for wear.

There was a public outcry in Hythe and the district with protests, petitions and public meetings calling for action. Hythe had had a ferry service to Southampton for generation upon generation; this one was not going to be the one that saw its end.

In April 2017, Blue Funnel Ferries took control of the Hythe – Southampton Ferry, Hythe Pier and the Hythe Pier Railway and immediately set about restoring the service and its assets to that expected. The travelling public responded. It was clear, however, particularly after the loss of its subsidy in April 2019, that the ferry proprietor could not do it all.

The Hythe Pier Heritage Association formed from the dissatisfaction and anger of 2016 set about raising the funds required for the restoration of the pier and the railway, with the aim to leave Blue Funnel to run the ferry. Acquiring charity status, the organisation has promoted numerous imaginative events to which the Hythe public have enthusiastically bought into. The most popular of these has been a music festival, "Rock the Pier", which in both 2018 and 2019, aided by fine warm sunny weather, attracted large numbers, raising many thousands of pounds for the cause.

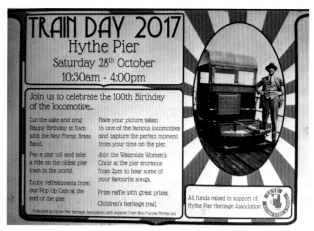

Train Day 2017 poster

To mark the centenary of the tractor units, the HPHA celebrated with "Train Day 2017". Despite the October chill, a large turn-out enjoyed rides on the train, a children's heritage trail, an exhibition of historic photographs, admission to the workshops and sheds, a pop-up café at the pierhead and a rendition of "Happy Birthday" as a centenary cake was cut. The event also attracted narrow gauge railway enthusiasts from far and wide.

THE HEARTBEAT OF HYTHE

100 YEARS AND BEYOND

As we human beings go through life, the years take their toll. Bits fail, modern medicine replaces hip and knee joints, even vital organs, kidney, liver, and heart. Apart from a shot of Botox, however, our outside appearance cannot defy the ravages of time. So, it is with our beloved Hythe Pier train.

New wheels October 2019 (Alan Titheridge)

As detailed in the previous chapter, White Horse Ferries replaced those bits that failed; Blue Funnel have continued to do likewise as in October 2019, when two bogie sets of two pairs of wheels and axles arrived back in Hythe having been sent to and machined by Alan Keef Ltd, a company in Ross-on-Wye that specialises in working on narrow gauge railways, at a cost of £3,400. The tractors and carriages, which have spent their lifetime in the open, exposed to wind and rain, snow, and ice and occasionally some scorching temperatures, are likewise struggling to withstand these ravages of time. It is clear to anyone looking at the train in 2021 that it is in desperate

Carriage 4 Bogie undergoing refurbishment, October 2019 (Alan Titheridge)

Carriage 4 undergoing refurbishment, October 2019 (Alan Titheridge)

need of some tender loving care and that urgent action is required to preserve and protect it to ensure its continued operation.

Alan Keef Ltd have a long association with the Hythe Pier Railway, having been involved with all aspects of its maintenance and repair of the track, bogies and wheels for almost a half-century. In early 2020 the Hythe Pier Heritage Association engaged the company with Mr Patrick Keef, its managing director and an acknowledged and well-respected narrow gauge railway engineer as a consultant, in preparation of the planned restoration of the train and track. Mr Keef's input would be to provide advice and support including the undertaking of survey work and the inspection of all work undertaken in the project.

Early in 2020, the Hythe Pier Heritage Association set about putting into being a project to fully restore each of the four carriages and both the remaining two tractor units with a timeline of two years to coincide with the centenary of the train operating on Hythe Pier in July 2022.

Specialist companies were to be invited to tender for the engineering aspect of the project; this to include the carriage base and bogie frames, bearings, springs, axles, and wheels. The carriage restoration would be conducted in collaboration with the Hythe Shed (at the Pier), a multi-skilled community group based on the Quay behind Hotspur House. Under the auspices of the Hythe Pier Heritage Association the project would be managed by Tina Brown, a member of the Hythe Pier Heritage Association board. Working closely with Blue Funnel, which would continue to operate the Hythe Pier Railway, to minimise any disruption of its operation, restoration was scheduled to commence in March 2020.

Blue Funnel passed ownership of Carriage No. 4 to the Hythe Pier Heritage Association at the end of February 2020 which enabled it to be able to undertake the commencement of work. The ferry company would still be responsible for the extensive engineering repairs to the carriage frame and bogies, including axles and wheels, whilst the carriage bodywork would become the responsibility of the Hythe Pier Heritage Association. With the help of the original drawings and plans, restoration on Carriage No. 4, which had been sitting in the workshop at the pier entrance since 2017, was all set to commence.

Firstly, a little understanding of the construction of the carriage. The timber flooring sits on cross members upon the carriage base supporting three compartments of slatted seating built on timber frames. The carriage side panel which would always be on the south side of the pier has three large picture windows, whilst that that would always face the north side of the pier has six smaller window panels, one each side of three glazed sliding doors which are hung from slide rails. The end panels support the roof along with periodic radial cross members. The roof is of plywood, moulded over the end and radial supports with a weatherproofing fibreglass sheath (added by White Horse Ferries in 2002).

The original hand-built coachwork appears to have been undertaken without too much emphasis on dimensional tolerance. Each carriage is slightly different; each compartment within each carriage slightly different, too, making reuse of some of the better-preserved materials that much more difficult. The rebuilding of the deconstructed carriage would be carried out using a modular approach, the overall length of the carriage base allowing for three equal-size side frames to be built and fitted each side of the carriage between two specially constructed stand-alone end frames. Glazing would be from the outside using hardwood retention beading. The refurbished doors would be hung from newly sourced slide rails and runners. A floor runner would be fitted. The scope of work planned for the floor-pans to be returned to their original design with timber boards and skirting, dispensing with the comparatively recent addition of aluminium chequer plate. All seating would be reused in the restoration. The roofing, once removed, would be inspected for possible re-installing.

Between November 23 and December 1, 1940, the German Luftwaffe conducted the most intense of the 57 bombing raids on Southampton made during World War II. As the bombs dropped, the Hythe ferry service continued. Ferry skipper Wilf Banks, many years later, recalled that when he took the first boat across (from Hythe) on what should have been a dark winter's morning after the night of the blitz of Southampton, fires from Hythe and Marchwood right around to

Southampton lit up Southampton Water like day. The Hythe Ferry carried on defiantly, the Hythe Pier train delivering and collecting its passengers did so, too.

Eighty years later there was a silent killer on the loose that managed what Reichsmarschall Georing was unable to do. The pandemic virus known as Covid-19 brought the world to its knees. On March 23, 2020, the United Kingdom was put into lockdown. Businesses not deemed vital were closed, the public told to stay at home. Blue Funnel continued to operate the ferry but as the local community and tourists alike followed the Government's advice and passenger numbers fell alarmingly, the operator succumbed and suspended the service.

Blue Funnel Ferries director Lee Rayment said at the time: "The Company can no longer support the service with the drastic drop in passenger numbers. We would love to continue but cannot financially maintain the service. Hopefully, these unprecedented times will ease in the near future and we can return to some form of normality."

And so, on April 18, 2020, the "Heartbeat of Hythe" fell silent.

Earlier, on March 28, 2020, the Hythe Pier Heritage Association had also suspended its activities. Peter King, on behalf of the Association, explained: "Like any responsible organisation we need to take the steps to reduce the risk in what we do in order to reduce the spread of Coronavirus."

This situation at first threatened and subsequently derailed the target completion date and, with it, potential fundraising events. Severe weather had already forced the cancellation of the Heritage Day event in October 2019 and "Spring into Action" scheduled for May 2020 had already been cancelled owing to the Coronavirus outbreak before, despite easing of restrictions, the highly popular (and accordingly highly lucrative source of revenue) music festival "Rock the Pier" fell victim, too. However, this did not stop fundraising altogether. An online quiz organised and staged by David and Jan Morris, using the Hythe and Waterside People Facebook site, brought in £245 of donations from appreciative participants.

On April 24, 2020, Peter King, was able to announce "significant financial support" with a grant of £10,000 from the Beaulieu Beaufort Foundation, a charity based in Bucklers Hard, Beaulieu, Hampshire, established in 2008 to support aspiring individual and grass-roots community projects. Peter King said: "This is a great start to our funding campaign to support the restoration of our historic and much-loved pier railway. We are very grateful to the Beaulieu Beaufort Foundation for their support and endorsement of our plans."

He added: "These funds will be used to buy the materials we need to begin the work to rebuild the railway carriages which are in a poor state of repair. The work will begin once the current restrictions imposed due to the Covid 19 Coronavirus crisis have been lifted."

The Hythe Ferry resumed operation, limited at first, on Saturday June 27, 2020; its passengers being carried to the boats along the pier by the Hythe Pier Railway. Resumption of the familiar clickety-clack soundtrack to life in Hythe, like the first cuckoo of spring, raised spirits throughout the village.

On July 22, 2020, Allan Fairhead, local councillor, and founder of the Shed (at the Pier) and his fellow volunteers offered up the first softwood trial frame against Carriage 4. Delivery of the timber for the restoration arrived on July 31. Because of its renowned durability and rich coloured grain, the timber chosen was Iroko, sometimes referred to as African Teak. The first "glued and screwed" Iroko frame was successfully offered up on September 9. Work continued steadily. Further frames were constructed, and skins of marine plywood were affixed. The seats and doors were removed to be worked on at a separate location nearby.

All hopes of completion by Christmas, however, were extinguished when Southampton, which had been less affected by the Government's Tier System for local lockdowns, was ordered into Tier 4 lockdown on November 5, restricting close association.

A national lockdown was enforced on January 6, 2021, one day after the BBC featured the work being carried out by HPHA and the Shed (at the Pier) in its local news programme "South Today".

Volunteers had been able to continue working remotely under Tier 4 restrictions. The skins were painted Moss Green (RAL 6005), seating was restained, and new lighting and window glass was fitted.

Easing of national restrictions came into being on April 12, 2021. HPHA rolled Carriage 4 out of the workshop on April 14, the first time it had been out in the open in four years. Protective shrink-wrapping was carried out in advance of an application of a new glass-fibre coating of the carriage roof. Subsequently "H P R" insignia was applied; but for a brief spell at the beginning of the 21st Century, not seen on the carriages since the early 1960s.

All this was happening under a black cloud of doubt. The ferry service, which had had many financial scares in recent years, had "run out of money". Having had no income for much of the previous year, Lee Rayment explained: "(Blue Funnel Ferries) have nothing left to get it going again."

In late February 2021, local resident Ashleigh Mutimear launched an online Crowdfunder appeal which the local community bought into, and local councils pledged emergency financial support. The campaign went on to raise more than £30,000, boosted by a 24-hour pier walk by Ashleigh Mutimear and Sonny Wilson, and the proceeds of a

children's book by Simon Chadwick, enabling Blue Funnel to make a limited restart of the Hythe Ferry on May 29, 2021.

On the same day, the Hythe Pier Heritage Association were finally able to put Carriage 4 back on track.

Carriage 4 back on track (Alan Titheridge)

Tractor 16307, which had been jointly repaired and restored by Blue Funnel Ferries and HPHA in conjunction with the Shed (at the Pier) and donated to HPHA, was also returned to the rails in a ceremony over the May Bank Holiday weekend.

Gerald Yorke's grandson Nigel Hasted performing the naming ceremony for tractor 16307 (Penny Wade)

In recognition of his contribution to the development and installation of the Hythe Pier Railway almost 100 years previous, 16307 was named Gerald Yorke in a short ceremony performed by Gerald Yorke's grandson Nigel Hasted and granddaughter Sara Richardson, with a cast plaque affixed to the front of the tractor.

The Hythe Pier Heritage Association will continue with its fundraising campaign to restore Hythe's jewel, its historic

Tractor 16307 restored and named after Gerald Yorke (Alan Titheridge)

pier and railway, in the face of whatever is thrown at it, because it and the community of Hythe and district believe "together we can".

The "Heartbeat of Hythe" has a future and will continue to be heard across Southampton Water for generations to come.

ACKNOWLEDGEMENTS

I would particularly like to thank Sath Naidoo of Blue Funnel Ferries for his valuable assistance and patience when I kept coming back with yet another question. Thanks, also, to James Percy of the General Estates Company for giving me unfettered access to its archive of historic letters and documents. I must also acknowledge help from Lee Rayment, the owner of Blue Funnel Ferries, Peter King, former chairman of the Hythe Pier Heritage Association, Graham Parkes of Waterside Heritage and Mr John Parry of Parry People Movers. Among the many individuals (in alphabetical order) who have proffered information, Diane Edge, Martin Ford, Scott Flood, John Greenwood, Nigel Hasted, Martin Haywood, Sarah Marsden, Anne Omissi, John Pipe, Alan Rowland, Peter and James Smith, Pauline Smith and Paul Wathan. Further, I am indebted to Simon Chadwick of Ceratopia Books for his contribution in the publication of this book and to Patrick Keef of Alan Keef Limited for his support in writing the foreword.

If I have omitted anyone, it is completely accidental, and I most sincerely apologise.

Photographs used in this book have been located from a variety of sources. Where obtained from the original photographer, organisation, or collection an acknowledgment has been attached. Some have come into my possession through other means but despite determined attempts to trace their origin some remain anonymous. If any photograph has accordingly been used without due credit I sincerely apologise. Should any reader believe this to be, please advise me and a credit will be added on any subsequent use.

*General Estates Co. Ltd Hythe Pier Railway, 27th September 1952, J H Meredith
(Alan Titheridge collection)*

Tractors 16302 and 16307, May 2017 (Alan Titheridge)

SOURCES OF REFERENCE

Much of the information drawn upon for this book has been from my extensive personal collection of research findings gathered in preparation for my earlier books, ephemera, memorabilia, and artefacts. Among other publications that have provided either substantial or just a snippet of information are: "The Hythe – Southampton Ferry including Hythe Pier Railway" by W. A. Stearn and Bert Moody published by Eltrac Publications in 1962, "The Hythe Pier Railway" by Peter A. Harding published by Peter A. Harding in 2009, "Hythe – A Waterside Village" by Graham Parkes published by Waterside Heritage in 2016, Brush Battery Locomotive by David Halfpenny 2006, historic copies of newspapers including the Hampshire Advertiser, Hampshire Independent, Southampton Times, Southern Evening and Daily Echo, the Lymington Times and local free publications including the Herald and the New Forest Post.

THE HEARTBEAT OF HYTHE

THE AUTHOR

I have spent the greater part of my life living in Hythe, including most of my youth. I grew up in Hythe. As a boy I would spend hours on the Hythe shoreline or at the end of the Hythe Pier watching the great liners making their way in and out of Southampton Docks, the origin of my lifelong passion for ships. At the end of the pier, I was fascinated with the movements of the ferry boats and from an early age they and the pier and train became special for me.

Alan Titheridge

Having been away from Hythe for a decade and a half, I am back to where I know I belong. I love this place. The pier and its train were not in the best of shape when I came back in 2016 but that could be about to change; my spirits so deflated when I first walked back down the Pier now lifted as plans for renovation are a real possibility. Generations have walked the pier or ridden the railway to get to the ferry boats; generations more will hopefully do the same.

I am retired now, like my 70th birthday my working days behind me, living with my wife Anne in Butts Ash. I am grateful for the years I have had, years denied my father and younger brother, both taken much too early. This is my time, a time to enjoy with Anne, my daughter Emma and granddaughter Calleigh.

I do have interests away from the water. I enjoy reading, both classic literature (the subject I excelled at during my education) and more modern novels. I write a little, not just about the Hythe Pier and Ferry. I

Alan Titheridge

have a very demanding garden, particularly during the autumn. I enjoy a good film. I am an avid supporter of Southampton Football Club and have suffered much disappointment over fifty plus years at the Dell and these days St Mary's with just the rare excursion to success. But, above all, I like to travel and have had the good fortune to have set foot on all the world's continents, Antarctica apart. I do much of my travelling by sea; it is the only way to go. Whenever I return from a trip, however, I get myself into Hythe. It is such a special place.

OTHER PUBLISHED WORK ON THE HYTHE PIER AND FERRY BY ALAN TITHERIDGE

BOOKS

Hythe Pier and Ferry – A History by Alan Titheridge
First edition published by Itchen Printers Ltd June 1981
ISBN 0 9507620 0 8
Second edition published by Itchen Printers Ltd April 1986
ISBN 0 9507620 0 8
Third edition published by Ferry Publications May 2019
ISBN 978-1-911268-29-1

ARTICLES

A Tribute to the Hythe Ferry by Alan Titheridge
Published in "Sea Breezes" magazine published by The Journal of
Commerce and Shipping Telegraph Limited September 1974

Hythe Ferry by Alan Titheridge
Published in A History of Ships (partwork) Issue 85 of 96 1985
published by New English Library

Also Available From Ceratopia Books

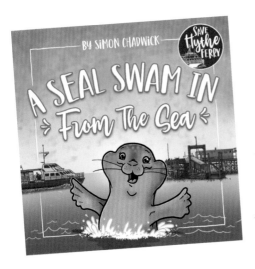

A Seal Swam In From The Sea

Written & illustrated by Simon Chadwick

The story of a lonely seal looking for friendship as she swims from the Solent to Hythe Pier. A delightful children's picture book inspired by the regular seal sightings off of Hythe, Hampshire, and featuring many local landmarks.

Chickens In Your Garden: Your Essential Guide To Keeping Chickens At Home

Written by Bryan Pass

With over 50 years of experience raising chickens, this is Bryan Pass's practical guide, full of straightforward, easy to follow advice. Accompanied by colourful cartoon illustrations, it's the only book you'll need to help you plan, choose, and look after your chickens.

www.ceratopiabooks.co.uk